THE
UNITED STATES
IN THE
CIVIL WAR

D1712062

Books by Don Lawson

The Young People's History of America's Wars Series

THE
UNITED STATES
IN THE
CIVIL WAR

BY

Don Lawson

Illustrated with photographs, and
maps and drawings by Robert F. McCullough

ABELARD-SCHUMAN
New York

Library of Congress Cataloging in Publication Data   Lawson, Don.   The United States in the Civil War.   Bibliography: p.   Includes index.   SUMMARY: Follows the events of the Civil War from the first shots at Fort Sumter to the signing of the surrender at the Appomattox Court House.   1. United States—History—Civil War, 1861–1865—Juv. lit. [1. United States—History—Civil War, 1861–1865]   I. Title.
E468.L39   973.7   76–54932
ISBN 0–200–00176–0

10   9   8   7   6   5   4   3   2   1

To the memory of my wife's grandfather

CORPORAL ANDREW EVANS YATES

U.S.A. 1861–1865

Acknowledgments

The author wishes to thank Margaret Parret for the use of the Civil War diary kept by her grandfather, Captain Orange Parret, 77th Illinois Infantry, during the entire course of the war.

Thanks are also due Nancy and Robert Evans for the use of Evans family letters written by Corporal John Remley, 28th Iowa Infantry, during the Vicksburg and lower Mississippi River campaigns.

The Department of the Army's chief of information, the National Archives, and the Library of Congress have also been most helpful in supplying photographs and special information.

Once again Robert McCullough has performed above and beyond the call of duty in preparing the several war maps.

And a special note of appreciation is offered to Elizabeth Slack for typing the final manuscript.

—D. L.

Contents

Illustrations

MAPS

*"I am tired and sick of war.
Its glory is all moonshine.
It is only those who have
neither fired a shot nor
heard the shrieks and groans
of the wounded who cry aloud
for blood, more vengeance,
more desolation. War is hell."*

—General William Tecumseh Sherman

FORT SUMTER— THE FIRST BLOW

On a warm sunny morning in the spring of 1861 two Confederate soldiers in a small boat flying a flag of truce were rowed out to Fort Sumter, a United States Federal fort in the middle of the harbor at Charleston, South Carolina. The American Civil War had not yet begun, but South Carolina had already seceded (withdrawn) from the United States and had demanded that Northern military forces be removed from Fort Sumter.

The two soldiers were carrying a note from Brigadier General P. G. T. Beauregard, Southern commander of the Charleston harbor defenses. Major Robert Anderson, commander of the Federal forces within Fort Sumter, received Beauregard's messengers. The note they bore demanded that Anderson and his men surrender the fort immediately. It read: "All proper facilities will be afforded for the removal of yourself and command, together with company arms and property, to any post in the United States which you may select. The flag which you have upheld so long and with such fortitude, under the most trying circumstances, may be saluted by you on taking it down."

Major Anderson read the surrender demand, sorrowfully noting General Beauregard's signature. Some years before, when Beauregard had been a student at West Point, Anderson had been his artillery instructor. Anderson was now about to test his former student's professional military skills. Although he hated the thought of the war that he knew was about to begin, Anderson had made the army his life for almost half a century and acted always out of a sense of soldierly duty. He had already written President Abraham Lincoln: "We shall strive to do our duty in defending Fort Sumter, but I frankly say that my heart is not in the war which I see is to be thus commenced."

Now Anderson replied to Beauregard's surrender demand: "I regret that my sense of honor and my obligations to my government prevent my compliance with your request."

The messengers took Anderson's reply and returned with it to General Beauregard. As Anderson watched them go, he knew the final die had been cast.

Shortly before dawn on Friday, April 12, 1861, the more than seventy guns from Beauregard's shore batteries, manned and supported by more than 40,000 Confederates, opened fire on the har-

The interior of Fort Sumter during bombardment. (LIBRARY OF CONGRESS)

bor fortress. Following a signal shot at 4:30 A.M., the honor of pulling the lanyard of the Confederate gun that fired the first shot of the war went to sixty-seven-year-old secessionist Edmund Ruffin from Virginia. Fort Sumter's forty-eight guns, manned by eighty-five Federal officers and men, did not reply until well after dawn at about 7:30 A.M.

The siege lasted for thirty-four hours. During its course Charleston citizens lined the shore of the harbor and stood on rooftops to watch the fireworks display provided by the more than 4,000 shells fired by Confederate gunners into the fortress. Anderson's men, however, were almost completely protected by the fort's stone casemates and suffered few serious casualties.

But Fort Sumter itself was soon so severely damaged and so filled with smoke that its defenders could scarcely see to continue to fire their few remaining undamaged guns. Once, after a lull in firing from the fort, Confederate troops cheered when the beleaguered garrison was able to renew its futile defensive firing from its six remaining guns. And at a point in mid-siege the fort's Stars and Stripes were shot down, making the Confederates think the Federal troops were about to surrender. But a Federal enlisted man soon nailed the flag back up, and the siege guns resumed their bombardment.

At best, however, Anderson's surrender of the fort was a foregone conclusion. Finally, on Saturday, April 13, Anderson agreed to the original surrender terms. And it was only then that the first serious casualties occurred.

General P. G. T. Beauregard. (LIBRARY OF CONGRESS)

The formal surrender ceremonies took place on Sunday, April 14. While Anderson's men were firing a fifty-gun salute to their flag, a pile of live cartridges was accidentally exploded, wounding five Federal soldiers and killing Federal private Daniel Hough—the war's first fatality. Hough was buried at the fort with services conducted by a Confederate chaplain accompanied by an honor guard of South Carolina volunteers.

Following the surrender ceremonies within Fort Sumter, the garrison was ferried to shore. There, with drums beating and colors flying, they marched between rows of Confederate troops lining the wharves, their hats in their hands as a token of respect for their defeated fellow soldiers. Later the garrison was allowed to sail north aboard a Federal steamer, the *Ysabel.*

But despite the gentlemanly manner in which the siege and surrender of Fort Sumter had been conducted, the incident marked the beginning of what would prove to be perhaps the saddest as well as the most savage military conflict in American history. For Beauregard's guns firing over Fort Sumter announced the opening act in that most bitter of all of so-called civilized man's conflicts, a civil or brother-against-brother war.

FIREBELL
IN THE NIGHT

Fort Sumter had been just one of four Federal forts in the South still manned by Union forces in the spring of 1861. The other three, all off the coast of Florida, were Pickens at Pensacola, Taylor at Key West, and Jefferson in the Dry Tortugas. President Lincoln had been seeking some way to unite the northern states of the United States against the southern states who had been threatening to withdraw from the Union and thus destroy it. Lincoln felt sure that a southern attack on any one of these forts might provide the means he was seeking to unify the North. He was right. For just as the Japanese attack on Pearl Harbor was to unite America against the Axis powers in the future World War II, so the firing upon and capture of Fort Sumter—although not in any way a surprise attack—united the North against the South in the Civil War.* The

*See another book in this series, *The United States in World War II*.

surrender of Fort Sumter did indeed electrify and unite the North as no other event had succeeded in doing up to this time.

The American Civil War had been smoldering and threatening to burst into flame for generations before the spring of 1861. Its causes lay deep in the grain of a rapidly growing America, beginning perhaps as far back as when the first black slaves had been imported into the country from Africa. The problems of slavery—both moral and economic—had haunted even the nation's Founding Fathers. Thomas Jefferson—himself a slaveowner—may have expressed it best when he said, "The momentous question, like a firebell in the night, awakened and filled me with terror."

It should be made clear, however, that the slavery question did not actually start the American Civil War. When the war began, the North fought to preserve the Union, and the South fought to become an independent nation. It was not until more than a year later that the slavery question was directly introduced into the conflict with the publication of President Lincoln's Emancipation Proclamation on January 1, 1863. This proclamation meant freedom for all slaves if the North won the war, while slavery would remain legal in the Confederate states if the South won. Nevertheless, as both Northern and Southern historians have pointed out, while the problem of slavery did not literally start the war, there probably would not have been a war without it.

Blacks were first brought from Africa to America in 1619 by a Dutch slave ship. Despite some colonists' objections to it, slavery almost immediately began to flourish, especially in the South. It was Jefferson who observed that "in a warm climate no man will labor for himself who can make another labor for him." Actually, however, slavery flourished in the South rather than in the North not because of the difference in climate but for economic reasons. The North was far more heavily industrialized, and its farms were relatively small as compared with the huge farm plantations of the South. Cotton farming and the raising of tobacco and sugar cane in the South called for large labor forces. Morality aside, unpaid slaves were ideal for this situation.

The British became the main dealers in African slaves in the eighteenth century, and America was the main market for these human cargoes of what was often inhumanely called "black ivory." Many American ship captains from the North also engaged in the trade.

When the United States Constitution was written and adopted, it both recognized and protected slavery. Nevertheless, the moral question of the right of one human being to "own" another continued to be raised in both the North and the South, and by early in the nineteenth century—1808—it became illegal to import slaves from Africa. Most people thought that slavery would thus eventually die out everywhere in the country and the problem would solve itself. But a few years earlier, in 1793, Eli Whitney had invented the cotton gin, and the Southern cotton kingdom began to flourish as never before.

Eli Whitney was a young man who had just graduated from Yale when he visited the South for the first time in 1792. There he heard Southern planters discussing the problem of removing seeds from cotton so it could be spun into cloth. It took twenty slaves at least a day to remove the seeds from twenty pounds of cotton.

Young Whitney had never seen any raw, unspun cotton before, but his inventive mind was challenged by the problem. The plantation on which he was staying had a small machine shop, and after some months of work there he perfected his device —a simple box containing a revolving wooden cylinder on which metal "fingers" clawed the seeds from the cotton without breaking its fibers.

Whitney made little or no money from his invention. Although he patented it in 1794, he received few royalties for the many copies of the gin that were made. He did, however, make money ($135,-000, or about $1 million in today's figures) on a new gun with parts that could be exactly duplicated in assembly-line fashion. Until 1798, when Whitney's gun with standardized parts was developed, muskets had been handmade. Out of Whitney's method grew mass production and the American factory system, with one person specializing in making or assembling a certain interchangeable part of a product.

By 1800, as a result of the cotton gin, cotton production had grown from 3,000 to 75,000 bales a year. In the next decade production grew to 5 million bales a year. Between 1800 and the start of the Civil War in 1861 the value of cotton exports grew from about $5 million (roughly $45 million in today's money) to about $190 million (about $1.75 billion today). Some 4 million slaves were employed in producing this enormous export crop.

During this period, which has often been called the South's Golden Age, grand Greek-style mansions were built on huge, prosperous plantations and life for the Southern white man, if not for his black slaves, was presumably lived out in what seemed like an eternity of sun-washed afternoons. The truth of the matter was, however, that even after the invention of Eli Whitney's cotton gin most Southern white people owned no slaves and received little or no financial returns for the cotton that was raised and sold abroad by perhaps a third of the Southern population. The great majority of Southern whites lived on poor, nonproductive lands, and their farms produced barely enough to feed and clothe their families. More often that not they lived not in porticoed mansions but in rude cabins built from pine logs. Rather than being prosperous enough to own slaves, they themselves were slaves to the soil from which they eked out a bare subsistence. In 1861 the population of the South was about 12 million, one-quarter of whom were black slaves owned by less than 400,000 whites.

Slavery first became a national political issue in

1818. It was then that Missouri requested to join the Union, and there was great debate over whether Missouri should be admitted as a slave state or a free state. By the Compromise of 1820 Missouri was admitted as a slave state, but it was agreed that in the future there would be no new slave states admitted north of Missouri's southern boundary.

As a result of the Mexican War, the United States acquired a vast expanse of new territory.* Even before the war ended in 1848 the debate was renewed over whether slavery should be allowed in the new territory. During the war Congressman David Wilmot had introduced an amendment to an appropriations bill that stated slavery would not be allowed in any territory acquired from Mexico. The amendment, called the Wilmot Proviso, was passed by the House of Representatives but rejected by the Senate, which had a majority of Southerners.

Out of the failure of the Wilmot Proviso, however, grew the Compromise of 1850, engineered by the aging but still effective statesman Senator Henry Clay, a Southerner who had fought unsuccessfully for half a century to abolish slavery. According to Clay's proposed compromise, California would be admitted to the Union as a free state, New Mexico and Utah would become territories with an option to choose between becoming slave or free states when admitted to the Union, and the slave trade would be abolished in the District of Columbia. In

*See another book in this series, *The United States in the Mexican War.*

return for these apparent concessions, the South was to be granted a stronger fugitive slave law. After a congressional debate of eight months the Compromise of 1850 was passed, but instead of bringing permanent peace between the North and South it simply postponed the Civil War for a few years.

One of the main reasons for the failure of the Compromise of 1850 to maintain peace was the strengthened fugitive slave law. The original Fugitive Slave Act had been passed in 1793. It provided for the return of escaped black slaves from one state or territory to another state or territory, but by 1850 this law was seldom enforced. The Fugitive Slave Act of 1850 not only revived the earlier law but also added severe penalties for anyone aiding in the escape of a slave or interfering with the return of a slave to his original owner. In response, many Northern states adopted Personal Liberty Laws. These laws prohibited Northern law officers from enforcing the revived Fugitive Slave Act.

The Personal Liberty Laws were sponsored by Northern *abolitionists*—people who fought to abolish slavery. One of their leaders was William Lloyd Garrison, who accused slaveowners of being Christian sinners. While many Northerners rallied to Garrison and his abolitionist crusade, Southerners united against him. The outright abolition of slavery, they said, would cause the economy of the South to collapse.

Another abolitionist, and a much more effective one, was Harriet Beecher Stowe, whose novel about slavery, *Uncle Tom's Cabin,* was published in 1852 and sold more than a million copies by the start of the Civil War. Mrs. Stowe's dramatic antislavery story rallied even greater support for runaway slaves and increased activity on the so-called Underground Railway. This was not an actual railway but a network of Northern homes and hiding places where runaway slaves were secretly kept until they could escape into Canada.

So important was *Uncle Tom's Cabin* among the events that led up to the tragic conflict between the North and the South that President Lincoln once said when he first met its author, "So this is the little lady who started this big war."

Among the final political events that triggered the war were the Kansas-Nebraska Act, sponsored by Illinois senator Stephen A. Douglas in 1854, and the Dred Scott decision handed down by the Supreme Court in 1857. Douglas' bill created the territories of Kansas and Nebraska and virtually repealed the Missouri Compromise. The people of Kansas and Nebraska were given the right to choose in favor of freedom or slavery when their territories became states, and fighting broke out between the proslavery and antislavery sides. In 1856 one antislavery fanatic, John Brown, and several of his sons led a raid in Kansas that resulted in the killing of several Southern settlers, and there were numerous other similar incidents in both of the new territories. Brown and his raiders were armed with "Beecher's Bibles." These were rifles named after the brother of Harriet Beecher Stowe, the Reverend Henry Ward Beecher, whose antislavery beliefs were so strong that he favored using rifles rather than Bibles to abolish the slave traffic.

The Dred Scott decision was a milestone Supreme Court ruling that declared a slave was not a citizen and had no civil rights. Scott was a black slave from the slave state of Missouri who had lived with his master for several years in the free state of Illinois and the free territory of Wisconsin. Back in Missouri, Scott sued for his freedom on the basis of having lived in free areas. Scott's suit, which finally reached the U.S. Supreme Court, was dismissed and the Missouri Compromise itself was declared unconstitutional. From that point on, war appeared to be inevitable.

In 1858 the prairie lawyer from Springfield, Illinois, Abraham Lincoln, ran for the United States Senate against the incumbent senator, Stephen A. Douglas. Douglas was a popular senator known as the "Little Giant" because he was short but had a powerful speaking voice. The tall, gaunt Lincoln and the short, red-faced Douglas engaged in a series of public arguments about slavery that became widely known as the Lincoln-Douglas debates. Although Douglas won reelection to the Senate, it was Lincoln who attracted national attention that was to lead to his nomination and election to the presidency two years later.

But in 1859 yet one more incident took place that brought war a step closer. The fanatical John

Brown led a raiding party, including not only his sons but also several blacks, on a Federal weapons and ammunition storage depot at Harpers Ferry, Virginia. The purpose of John Brown's raid was to seize arms and to encourage slaves to escape from their masters throughout the area. Brown and his raiders were driven off by a detachment of U.S. Marines led by the future Confederate general Robert E. Lee. Brown was wounded and captured and two of his sons were killed. Later in 1859 Brown was hanged for treason, murder, and inciting slaves to revolt. To many Northerners and most Southern slaves, Brown died a martyr to the antislavery cause. To Southern whites Brown was a symbol of what the North really wanted—a slave revolt that would result in mass murder of whites throughout the South. Interestingly, Robert E. Lee, then a U.S. Army colonel, was in charge of the military party that hanged Brown. One of the militiamen in the party was John Wilkes Booth, who would later assassinate Lincoln.

In 1860 the Republican party nominated Abraham Lincoln for president. The Democrats split into a Northern party and a Southern party, the Northerners nominating Douglas and the Southerners nominating John C. Breckinridge of Kentucky. With the split in the Democratic party, Lincoln won easily, the first Republican to become president.

Despite the fact that Lincoln had moderate views on the slavery question, the South thought he and his new Republican party would not respect their property rights—and they regarded their slaves as a part of their property. Interestingly, Lincoln had actually said in 1854 that he did not really know what to do about slavery. "I surely will not blame them [southern slaveowners] for not doing what I should not know how to do myself," Lincoln said. "If all earthly power were given me, I should not know what to do about this existing institution."

And in regard to the right of the Southern states to secede from the Union and create their own nation, Lincoln had said immediately after the Mexican War: "Any people anywhere, being inclined and having the power, have the right to rise up and shake off the existing government, and form a new one that suits them better. Any portion of such people that can may revolutionize and make their own of so much of the territory as they inhabit."

But most of the people of the South did not now recall having heard these words. Or if they did, they did not believe them. And in this perhaps they were right, for the new president—either for moral or political reasons or a combination of both—had now completely changed his mind and as commander in chief of the Union military forces was about to embark on a war that would be fought not only to preserve the Union but also to abolish slavery.

The South's reaction to Lincoln's election was swift. He would take office on March 4, 1861. (It was not until 1933 that the presidential inauguration date was changed from March 4 to January 20.) On December 20, 1860, South Carolina seceded from the Union. Mississippi, Alabama, Georgia, Florida,

Louisiana, and Texas soon joined South Carolina. And on February 8, 1861, representatives from the seceding states met at Montgomery, Alabama, and established the Confederate States of America. Jefferson Davis of Mississippi was elected president, and Alexander Stephens of Georgia was elected vice president.

The Civil War between the Confederate States and the United States began with the Confederate attack on Fort Sumter on April 12, 1861.

Confederate president Jefferson Davis. (LIBRARY OF CONGRESS)

THE CALL
TO ARMS

Despite the fact that the conflict had been brewing for months and even years, neither side was actually prepared to fight a war. Nor did either side expect the war to be a long one. Immediately after the surrender of Fort Sumter, President Lincoln was forced to call upon the loyal states of the Union to furnish 75,000 militiamen (an early form of National Guardsmen) to serve for three months—the length of time allowed by the law in all of the states. The response was enthusiastic.

Lincoln's action caused the slaveholding states of Virginia, North Carolina, Tennessee, and Arkansas to secede from the Union and join the Confederacy. The western part of Virginia remained loyal to the Union, thus becoming the state of West Virginia. All in all, eleven Southern states, with a population of 10 million—a third of them slaves—fought against twenty-three Northern states, with a population of 23 million.

The loss of Virginia to the Union also caused the loss of one of the regular U.S. Army's outstanding officers, Robert E. Lee. When war had first threatened, Lee was slated to become commander of the Union forces. But when Virginia seceded, Lee could not bring himself to fight against his native state. Lee was named a Confederate general, just one of about a third of the 1,100 U.S. Army officers to resign their commissions and join the Confederacy. None of the more than 15,000 regular U.S. Army enlisted men were allowed to resign.

Even before Lincoln was inaugurated, the president of the Confederacy, Jefferson Davis, another West Point graduate and former U.S. Army officer, had called for 100,000 volunteers to serve the South for a year. More than that number responded.

In the first few months of the war, Winfield Scott, general in chief of the Union army, warned Lincoln that the war would be a bigger and longer and bloodier affair than anyone anticipated. Consequently, Lincoln established forty regiments of U.S. Volunteers, or more than 40,000 men. These were to supplement the regular state militia and volunteered to serve until the war ended. Regular army volunteers enlisted for six years. Lincoln also increased the regular army by nine regiments, or more than 22,000 men, and added 18,000 men to the U.S. Navy. Response to the calls for volunteers was also enthusiastic, and men poured into training camps so fast that the Union War Department had to call for a slowdown in the induction of recruits. Eventually more than 1.5 million men wore the blue uniform of the Union Army and just under 1 million men wore Confederate gray. At the start of the war both sides depended upon volunteer forces, but by 1862 the South had to resort to a military draft and the North did so beginning in 1863.

While volunteers on both sides were more than ready and willing to get into combat they were far from professionally able. Most were such raw and untrained recruits that training officers almost despaired of ever getting them prepared for the rigors of war. Some men were so green that they had difficulty learning to drill because they could not tell their right foot from their left. To overcome this problem, some ingenious drill sergeant had the recruits tie pieces of hay to one ankle and pieces of straw to the other. He then barked out the command "Hay foot, straw foot!" rather than "Left, right!"

At the start of the conflict uniforms were frequently designed by the individual soldier. Often they were wildly colorful and intended for the parade ground rather than the battlefield. Each state militia also had a different style of uniform, and it was difficult for new officers not only to recognize their own troops but also to distinguish friend from foe. After several early battles in which there was great confusion because of these hodgepodge uniforms, regulation uniforms were adopted by both sides.

While worse than useless in the field, many of the colorful early uniforms had great appeal in the eyes of the public. In the White House, for example, President Lincoln's two small sons—Willie, eleven, and Tad, nine—were among those greatly taken with them. Shortly after the Civil War began, in fact, Willie and Tad acquired special uniforms of their own patterned after an Illinois volunteer regiment and organized a number of Washington boys and girls into a squad they called "Mrs. Lincoln's Zouaves."* The president himself, in the midst of the press of Civil War duties, managed several times to review this gaily garbed group of youngsters.

Before regulation uniforms were adopted another method of identification came to be the division patch or flash. This was devised by Philip Kearny, a colorful general who had lost an arm in leading a cavalry charge in the Mexican War. Greatly loved by the men who served under him, Kearny sought to instill pride in his troops by having them wear a red cloth patch on their caps. This insignia could not be worn, however, until the men had engaged in combat. The device was later adopted throughout the Union army, and out of it grew the shoulder patches or flashes worn by today's army and air force men and women.

In the beginning, most of the officers were as amateur at soldiering as the men they led, although this was more the case in the North than in the

*Certain volunteer regiments were called Zouaves mainly because they patterned their uniforms after colorful French infantry regiments of the same name.

South. Many were elected to their commands by the men who served under them, and not a few were appointed purely for political reasons. Consequently, discipline was extremely difficult to establish and maintain in both Northern and Southern armies. Men performed duties and went into combat action more or less because they wanted to, and when they did not want to they saw little wrong, nor did their fellow soldiers, in doing something else. It was not uncommon, on a long march for example, to find troops falling out of formation to forage in the countryside for fresh food. But finally, as early battles began to take their toll, the need for leadership and discipline became self-evident, and highly capable, professional officers and men emerged on both sides.

Food both in camp and in the field was always a problem. There were no such things as mess halls or field kitchens or company cooks. Instead, the men banded together in small units and perhaps one man was chosen as a cook. Each man was issued a weekly supply of meat, hardtack (hard biscuits), coffee, salt, and sugar, and these were either prepared individually or pooled and prepared by the man chosen as cook. Supplements to these "iron rations" were constantly sought by the men, so it was little wonder that they scoured the countryside when there was an opportunity for fresh fruit, vegetables, milk, game, and the like. Stomach problems were common, men dying not infrequently from dysentery, and scurvy was not unknown.

One of the South's major problems was how to provide weapons and ammunition for its troops. It had only about 150,000 small arms (rifles, muskets, and handguns), and only about 10,000 of these were modern weapons. All the rest were smoothbores and flintlocks dating back to the War of 1812 and the Mexican War. Smokeless powder was virtually unavailable. Nevertheless, when Southern soldiers volunteered they usually brought with them some sort of weapon—a shotgun or primitive rifle. The wide variety of weapons, of course, presented an additional problem—the need for a wide variety of ammunition. There was, however, a large ironworks at Richmond which was immediately assigned the task of producing weapons, and the South also was able to import guns and ammunition (from small arms and bullets to artillery guns and shells) from Europe in exchange for cotton. Cotton was in fact the South's "secret weapon" through most of the war, and it was sometimes said that cotton and courage were the two major resources of the Confederacy.

The North, on the other hand, had all the advantages on its side when it came to manufacturing any and all kinds of war needs or supplying its troops. At the start of the war there were more than 100,000 manufacturing plants in the North as compared with 18,000 in the South. The North's railway system also was far superior to that of the South, making it much easier to move and supply its troops. Not only did the North have twice as many miles of railroad as the South, but it also had the means of keeping these railroads in operation, while the South did not. The Civil War was the first major conflict in which railroads played the major role in transportation, so the North's advantage in this regard was vitally important.

At sea, the North was also immeasurably superior to the South, having most of the United States Navy at its command plus numerous private merchant ships. Since the South had to import most of its needed war materials and other supplies, it found itself at a constant disadvantage as its few ships plus those of European merchant fleets had to fight their way through the naval blockade established by President Lincoln early in the war and maintained throughout the conflict.

In the end it was the North's all but overwhelming advantages in manufacturing, availability of war materials, and number of men that finally defeated the Confederacy.

But in the beginning these advantages did not immediately become apparent, and for at least two years the end did not appear inevitable. In the beginning, in fact, it appeared that the South might defeat the North—and quickly. The first evidence of this occurred at a small town in northern Virginia called Manassas Junction near a creek called Bull Run. This was the first major battle of the Civil War.

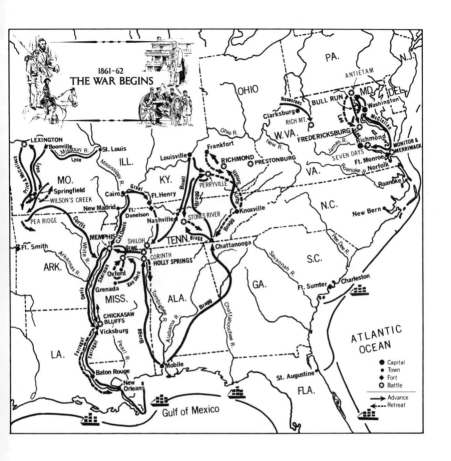

1861-62
THE WAR BEGINS

PA.

OHIO

ANTIETAM

Rosecrans
Clarksburg   BULL RUN   MD.   DEL.
RICH MT.   Washington   McClellan
W.VA.   FREDERICKSBURG   Richmond

Ohio R.   New R.   James R.   MONITOR &
Frankfort   SEVEN DAYS   MERRIMACK
LEXINGTON   Louisville   RICHMOND   Ft. Monroe
Boonville   St. Louis   PRESTONBURG   Roanoke R.   Norfolk
Missouri R.   Lyon   VA.   Roanoke
Lyon   ILL.   KY.
MO.   Cairo   Grant   Ft. Henry   Buell   PERRYVILLE   N.C.
Springfield   New Madrid   Ft.   Nashville   Knoxville   New Bern
WILSON'S CREEK   Donelson   STONES RIVER
Curtis   Memphis   Chattanooga   Pee Dee R.
PEA RIDGE   White R.   TENN.   Bragg   S.C.
Ft. Smith   Arkansas R.   MEMPHIS   SHILOH   Savannah R.
Grant   CORINTH   Ft. Sumter   Charleston
Oxford   HOLLY SPRINGS
ARK.   Sherman   Van Dorn
Grenada   Tombigbee R.   GA.
MISS.   ALA.   Bragg
CHICKASAW   Alabama R.   Chattahoochee R.   ATLANTIC
BLUFFS   OCEAN
Vicksburg   Pearl R.   ● Capital
LA.   Bragg   ● Town
Baton Rouge   Mobile   ◆ Fort
Farragut   ✪ Battle
New Orleans   St. Augustine
FLA.   → Advance
Gulf of Mexico   ┅► Retreat

THE FIRST BATTLE OF BULL RUN

The South had one major advantage over the North throughout the war. This was the fact that it did not have to attack to win. If the South managed to successfully defend itself against attacks by the North, then the South would win. If the war became a stalemate, then the South would win. Fighting as it was for States' rights—the right, for example, of a state to secede from the Union if necessary to maintain racial segregation—the South had only to maintain its independence to prove its point. It was up to the North to force the seceding states back into the Union, and once war was declared this meant defeating them in battle. (The right of secession was, of course, only one part of the States' rights doctrine, which was intended to protect *all* of the rights and powers of the states against the rights and powers of the Federal government.)

Ironically, Confederate president Jefferson Davis himself did not believe in secession. Just a few months before Bull Run he wrote one of his sons: "Secession is nothing but revolution. Secession was termed treason by our first Virginia statesmen. What can it be now?" But in the same letter he concluded: "Still, a Union that can only be maintained by swords and bayonets, and in which strife and civil war are to take the place of brotherly love and kindness, has no charm for me." Reluctantly, perhaps more in love than in anger, Davis prepared to lead the defense of his beloved state and homeland. So it was throughout the South, except that Davis' fellow Southerners took up arms more in anger than in love.

Recognizing the fact that the North must attack to win, the U.S. War Department ordered the army to begin an offensive campaign early in July 1861. Army leaders complained that their recruits were not ready for combat, but the Washington authorities insisted upon action. A part of their reason was the fact that the militia's three-month term of enlistment was about to run out.

When Virginia seceded from the Union, the capital of the Confederacy was established at Richmond. This brought the rival capitals, Richmond and Washington, to within 100 miles of each other. While neither city was of prime military importance, both were important as far as public pride and morale were concerned. Northerners especially thought that if Richmond fell the South would fall, and "On to Richmond" became a Northern battle cry in the summer of '61.

Up until that time Union general in chief Scott

had planned on taking a year to prepare his armies for war. Veteran of the War of 1812 and the Mexican War, Scott did not believe in fighting battles with untrained amateur soldiers. Scott's long-range plans for the war were to fully train 100,000 men while a powerful naval blockade strangled Southern ports. Then the trained Union forces would advance into the South following the route of the Mississippi River, thus dividing and conquering the Confederacy. This elaborate scheme was laughed at by the press, which dubbed it Scott's "Anaconda Plan," after the huge South American snake that kills by coiling itself around its prey and strangling it. Eventually this was actually the plan that was mainly followed to win the war, but now the press and the public had no time for it. They wanted action, and bowing to public opinion, President Lincoln urged Scott to send his untrained troops into battle.

At the beginning of July 1861 there were some 50,000 Union troops in the Washington area. With the exception of several thousand regulars, these were virtually all untrained volunteers and militia. Their commander was Brigadier General Irvin McDowell. To defend Richmond, General Beauregard had 20,000 Confederates stationed at Manassas, just thirty miles from Washington. Manassas was a key road and railway junction important to both capitals. An additional 10,000 Confederate troops were stationed forty miles to the northwest in the Shenandoah Valley under Brigadier General Joseph E. Johnston. These were faced by 18,000

Union troops at Martinsburg near Harpers Ferry under Brigadier General Robert E. Patterson. Other small units, both Union and Confederate, were scattered throughout the area. McDowell decided to make his major move against Beauregard at Manassas. The battle took place on July 21, 1861.

When McDowell's army of 32,000 soldiers moved out from the Washington area, they were accompanied by a second army of hundreds of civilians—congressmen, newspapermen, and just plain sightseers. The sightseers even carried picnic baskets for the day's outing, at which they expected to see the Rebels easily whipped.

McDowell's plan was to attack the left flank of Beauregard's army, which was defending the main Manassas railway junction. This would prevent Beauregard from being reinforced with troops by rail from Johnston's command in the Shenandoah Valley. But spies in Washington reported McDowell's plan to Jefferson Davis in Richmond, and Davis sent a telegraph message to Johnston ordering him to immediately move out of the valley to Manassas. (The telegraph, like the railroad, played its first major military role in this war.) Aided by a cavalry screen set up by Colonel J. E. B. "Jeb" Stuart, Johnston managed to get almost 10,000 troops past Patterson's defenses and ship them by rail to Manassas, where they joined Beauregard and were ready for action when McDowell first attacked.

The first Union thrust at Sudley Springs beyond Bull Run Creek was late in getting started, but it

General Joseph Johnston. (LIBRARY OF CONGRESS)

went well. One brigade led by Colonel William Tecumseh Sherman crossed Bull Run early in the fighting and especially distinguished itself. Gradually the Confederates fell back to a high ridge just off the Warrenton turnpike (road) near two private homes, the Henry and Robinson houses. Inside the former an eighty-year-old woman, Judith Henry, was accidentally killed by Union shell fire and rifle bullets. (The involvement of the civilian population in the fighting was one of the "modern" aspects of the Civil War.)

Along the ridge the Confederates were rallied by Brigadier General Thomas J. Jackson, who earned his legendary nickname that day. As most of the Confederates continued to retreat, Jackson and his Virginia troops alone stood firm. A fellow Rebel general, Barnard Bee, who was killed almost before he got the words out of his mouth, saw Jackson's heroic stand and shouted to his own men: "There stands Jackson like a stone wall! Rally behind the Virginians!" The great Confederate general became Stonewall Jackson from that moment.

And from that moment the tide turned against the attacking Union forces. Their retreat was at first gradual and orderly. Then confusion set in as Confederate infantrymen and a unit of Confederate artillerymen dressed in blue uniforms (no standard uniform had yet been adopted and troops on both sides were confused between friend and foe throughout the battle) were mistaken for Union troops and allowed to advance virtually into the middle of the Union forces before they were recognized. When the Confederate infantry and artillery began firing at pointblank range against the Federal forces, near-panic resulted. The panic was somehow increased by the strange yell the Union forces now heard coming from the throats of their enemy. This was actually a fox-hunting cry, but the counterattacking Confederates had adopted it as a battle cry. The Rebel yell, now heard for the first time, was to be heard in battles throughout the war.

Adding to the confusion were the hundreds of civilians who got in the way of the retreating army. Soldiers stumbled over picnic baskets and became entangled in the slow-moving civilian hordes. Soon the cry went up "The cavalry are coming! The cavalry are coming!"—the Rebel cavalry led by Jeb Stuart was already becoming famed and feared— and soldiers and civilians all ran even faster to escape. This wild flight did not stop until McDowell's army straggled exhausted into Washington the following day.

As the Federal forces retreated toward the Northern capital, Stonewall Jackson, despite the fact that he had been wounded in the fighting, said to Jefferson Davis: "Give me 5,000 men and I'll capture Washington City tomorrow."

But Davis and the rest of the Confederate high command were temporarily content. They had won a first—and perhaps even final—smashing victory. Nevertheless, Davis cautioned his people against a false sense of security. He knew that the South's

General Thomas J. "Stonewall" Jackson. (U.S. SIGNAL CORPS
PHOTO, NATIONAL ARCHIVES, BRADY COLLECTION)

amateur troops, despite their overwhelming victory, had been as exhausted as the amateur troops of the North at the end of the fighting.

Almost 1,500 Union soldiers were taken prisoner, while only 8 Confederates surrendered. A comic touch was added when it was discovered that included among the bag of Northern prisoners was a New York congressman, Alfred Ely, who had strayed too near the fighting and failed to keep up with the wild Union retreat.

But there was nothing comic about the number of casualties. In dead, wounded, and missing the South had lost 2,000 men. Union casualties were even higher, numbering just under 3,000. Both sides regarded these figures as appalling, especially for a day's action that had started out as something of a lark.

The first amateur battle of the war had now been fought. The future conduct of the conflict would be in the hands of the professionals.

A GENERAL
WITH THE
"SLOWS"

The first thing the Confederates did after the First Battle of Bull Run was to change the design of their flag. Not only had the lack of standard uniforms been confusing on both sides (standard uniforms were now adopted), but the Confederate flag, the so-called Stars and Bars, had also frequently been mistaken for the Stars and Stripes. President Davis now ordered the adoption of what was to become the famous Southern battle flag with its highly visible Cross of St. Andrew.

The first thing President Lincoln did after the First Battle of Bull Run was to select a new commander for what he knew must be a new Northern army. This was General George B. McClellan—"Little Mac," who was the most promising young officer in the Union forces, the most beloved by his men, and finally, perhaps, the most disappointing leader the North was to have. A few months after McClellan

General George B. McClellan and his wife. (LIBRARY OF
CONGRESS)

was put in charge of the Army of the Potomac—as the Federal forces around Washington were called —General Scott retired from military service because of age and poor health and McClellan became general in chief of the Union forces.

McClellan was just thirty-four, a graduate of West Point, and a veteran of the Mexican War. Between that war and the Civil War he had resigned from the army to go into business, at which he had been very successful, becoming president of a railway in Ohio. After Fort Sumter the governor of Ohio had put McClellan in charge of all the state's volunteer troops with the rank of major general. While he was training these troops, a seedy-looking ex–infantry captain appeared at McClellan's headquarters looking for a job. The down-at-the-heels ex-infantryman was told to come back later, but he never did. Instead he returned to his home in Illinois, where he was put in charge of a regiment of that state's volunteers. He was Ulysses S. Grant, who was to go on to become the top Union general and would one day accept the South's final surrender at Appomattox Courthouse.

Before the Battle of Bull Run, McClellan had led his Ohio troops in what was actually a minor combat action in the western part of Virginia, where the Confederates were trying to recruit troops despite the fact that this part of Virginia was loyal to the Union. In May 1861 McClellan crossed the Ohio River and drove the Confederates out, a small feat of arms but one that enabled West Virginia to become a state. McClellan had been nationally praised for this first action of the war, and it was on the basis of this acclaim that Lincoln had selected him to lead all of the Northern armies after the rout at Bull Run. Later Little Mac was to say, quite accurately: "It probably would have been better for me personally had my promotion been delayed a year or more."

As his nickname indicated, Little Mac was a rather small man, but he was powerfully built and quite handsome. His combination of ramrod-straight military bearing and casual boyish charm led newspapermen to call him "the Young Napoleon," to which McClellan did not object in the least. He even adopted a Napoleonic pose for photographers.

Little Mac was definitely a military disciplinarian, and it was discipline that the Union's Army of the Potomac needed at this juncture if it was to regain its self-respect. The first thing he did was establish a military police unit that swept through the streets and taverns of Washington, clearing them of soldiers who were supposed to be in camp. In the camps themselves that surrounded Washington Little Mac ordered rigid daily inspections. Often he led these inspections himself, galloping into an encampment astride his huge black horse, Dan Webster, dismounting and slowly walking down the line of tents before which stood rows of men at rigid, parade-ground attention. His sharp eyes and white gloves missed very little. Shoes, rifles, equipment—all had to be spotless. When he was doubtful about what he saw, Little Mac would run a white glove over a mess kit or rifle, and if his glove was soiled disciplinary action swiftly followed. If his glove came away clean, the owner of the equipment was rewarded with a brief but heartwarming smile. The men loved it and him. Within two weeks Little Mac commented in a letter: "I have restored order completely."

Within a matter of two months he had completely restored the Army of the Potomac's pride in itself. The men's military training in the use of weapons and the method of going from column formation into battle lines was also gradually turning them into professional soldiers. Wherever Little Mac rode on Dan Webster, his men cheered him. And Little Mac always responded with a jaunty salute that made them love him even more. They were ready for anything; they would follow him anywhere. And it was right at that point that the first worm of doubt began to gnaw at President Lincoln about his newly appointed commander.

Lincoln, of course, had been enormously pleased at what a man of action General McClellan at first seemed to be. But as days became weeks and weeks became months and McClellan continued to prepare his troops for action without seeming to have specific plans for what that action was going to be, Lincoln grew doubtful and then impatient. At first he accused McClellan of having the "slows." Then he got even more bitingly sarcastic and commented that "if General McClellan did not plan on using his army, the President would like to borrow it for a while."

Despite the president's and the Northern public's growing impatience, there was very little further activity on the part of the Union armies in either the eastern or western theaters of war during 1861. The Confederates were, of course, content to remain in place, although Jefferson Davis had to turn down several plans put forward by his leading commanders for an all-out attack on Washington.

In October McClellan did make one minor military move, and it proved disastrous. This was in the wooded area of Ball's Bluff along the Potomac some thirty miles above Washington. McClellan had had reports of a concentration of Confederate troops at Ball's Bluff, and he sent several regiments of infantry to scout the Rebels and report back to him. Little Mac wanted to know what the Rebels were doing there. He did not intend the scouting mission to turn into a heavy combat action.

Nevertheless, the mission was not well planned, and the Northern reconnaissance detachment stumbled head-on into the alert Rebels and suffered severe casualties. Among those killed was a colonel of volunteers, Edward D. Baker. Baker had recently resigned from the Senate to join the volunteers and his sudden death caused a congressional investigation. Out of this inquiry grew the Joint Congressional Committee on the Conduct of the War, which was to give President Lincoln and his top generals nothing but headaches throughout the war.

The Army of the Potomac's winter quarters. (U.S. SIGNAL CORPS
PHOTO, NATIONAL ARCHIVES, BRADY COLLECTION)

As 1861 drew to a close, it was little wonder that Lincoln had become somewhat desperate in his search for some good news as well as for a leader. That news was to come from out of the West in the form of a man who fought first, ready or not, and asked questions afterward.

"NO TERMS EXCEPT UNCONDITIONAL SURRENDER!"

"There is one West Pointer, I think in Missouri, little known, and whom I hope the northern people will not find out. I mean Sam Grant. I knew him well at West Point and in Mexico. I should fear him more than any of their officers I have yet heard of. He is not a man of genius, but he is clear-headed, quick and daring."

That was the comment made by Confederate brigadier general Richard Ewell when the Civil War began. Ewell's words had a curiously prophetic ring, because fortunately for the North the Union did find out about him.

Ulysses S. Grant had had an outstanding combat record as a young officer in the Mexican War, but life in the peacetime army bored him, and he resigned his commission and tried farming in Missouri. But civilian life also bored him, and he proved to be a bad farmer. After failing at a variety of jobs

General Ulysses S. Grant. (LIBRARY OF CONGRESS)

Grant drifted into the harness business at his father's store in Galena, Illinois. Here too he was no great success, but he did gain a reputation for being able to break and train horses, which he occasionally said he preferred to most people. Grant also gained a well-deserved reputation as a heavy drinker that he did little to dispute—until war began and there was fighting to do. Then the bottle disappeared.

Grant was far from self-confident, however, when the war first started. In fact, when the governor of Illinois, Richard Yates, appointed him a colonel in charge of a regiment of volunteers, Grant had more than a few doubts about his ability to lead them in combat. His men also had similar doubts about their colonel's ability when he first took command. His civilian clothes were patched and baggy. When he traded these for a uniform, the uniform usually looked as if he had slept in it. But in their first successful combat action against a small Rebel force in Missouri, Grant's men were tremendously impressed at the way he seemed to come to life at the first sign of action.

Grant seemed to be fearless—a presumption that was not true; he always said the enemy was as scared as he was, and that evened things up. But the astonishing thing about Grant was that although he was vague and uncertain in a peaceful situation, battle brought out all of his instinctive sense of command and authority. The sound of the guns seemed to send new life flowing through him, and his actions and commands were clear, positive, and somehow unerringly right. It was not that he always made the right decisions ahead of time, but once in a battle he seldom erred. And contrary to Ewell's comment about Grant's lack of genius, he did have a peculiar kind of genius: his swift-as-a-cobra's ability to take advantage of an enemy general's mistakes.

One of the most interesting things about Grant was that he never swore. In an age and an army where profanity was a common part of speech, Grant's strongest expression was "doggone." But there was never any mistaking his grim purpose when he gave an order. As Lincoln commented: "When Grant says jump, his men say 'how high?'"

Following Grant's minor but successful combat action in Missouri, he was made a brigadier general and stationed at Cairo, Illinois. This was a key to the western half of the Confederacy because it was only a few miles from Paducah, Kentucky, on the Ohio River, which controlled the mouths of the Tennessee and Cumberland rivers. These two rivers led directly into Alabama, Mississippi, and Tennessee, heartland of the western Confederacy. To defend them the Rebels had built Fort Henry on the Tennessee and Fort Donelson on the Cumberland.

Acting on his own initiative—like British field marshal Douglas Haig in World War I, Grant always had a "sincere desire to engage the enemy"—Grant captured Paducah. Kentucky had been hoping to remain neutral in the war, but this action placed the state squarely in the conflict. Throughout the Civil

War, however, Kentucky's loyalties remained divided between the North and the South, families often fighting against families.

After taking Paducah, Grant told his immediate commander, Major General Henry Halleck, that he planned to move against Fort Henry. Halleck, who was aptly nicknamed "Old Brains," was quick to realize the importance of Grant's proposal and gave his approval.

A fleet of armored gunboats plus other transport craft carried Grant's 15,000 men up the Tennessee. The ironclad gunboats, an invention of civilian James B. Eads, who had never been paid for them, were under the command of Navy commodore Andrew Foote. Foote landed Grant's troops near Fort Henry and proceeded with his gunboats to within firing distance of the fort. As Grant's troops moved overland through bad weather and difficult country, Foote's ironclads began to shell Fort Henry on February 6, 1862. Within a few hours the Confederate commander, Brigadier General Lloyd Tilghman, surrendered, and the Stars and Stripes were flying over Fort Henry by the time Grant and his troops arrived. But before the surrender most of the fort's defenders had fled to Fort Donelson just ten miles east on the Cumberland.

Grant did not care who had won the race to capture the fort. The fact that it had been taken was the main thing. He immediately telegraphed Halleck: "Fort Henry is ours. I shall take and destroy Fort Donelson on the 8th." According to one story,

Grant then cut his telegraph line to Halleck so that his initiative could not be countermanded.

But Donelson was a somewhat tougher nut to crack than Henry, and Grant's timetable was off by more than a week.

First of all the Confederate theater commander, General Albert Sidney Johnston—no relation to the Brigadier General Joseph Johnston at Bull Run—was keenly aware that the fall of Fort Donelson could well mean the fall of Nashville and the overrunning of the whole of Tennessee. Johnston, now supported by General Beauregard, who had been sent from the East by McClellan, promptly sent 12,000 reinforcements to Donelson. This brought the total number of Rebel defense troops inside the fort to 17,500 men, but Grant, too, had been reinforced with some 10,000 troops from Halleck.

Grant's first move was to send Foote and his gunboats back to Cairo and then up the Cumberland to Donelson. Grant then led his 25,000 men eastward through a sea of mud created by a storm of snow and sleet that had descended on the area. The bad weather delayed the march, but Grant arrived at the fort on February 12. Foote and his gunboats had also arrived by this time, and they tried to force Donelson to surrender as Henry had by gunboat bombardment. Severe fire from the fort, however, damaged the gunboats so badly that they had to withdraw. Foote was wounded in this fighting.

Reluctantly, Grant now prepared to lay siege to the fort. But at this juncture Rebel forces tried to break out of Donelson and escape toward Nashville. The breakout attempt was at first successful, but Grant succeeded in rallying his men and forced the Confederates back inside the fort. That night the fortress commander, Brigadier General Simon Buckner, sent a message to Grant asking him for "the terms for capitulation."

Before the war Buckner and Grant had been close friends. In fact, when Grant had resigned from the army after the Mexican War, Buckner had loaned him money to pay his train fare home. Now, however, the two men were professional army enemies, and to Grant Buckner was merely the first Rebel general to ask for surrender terms from a Union general.

Grant's reply was terse and to the point: "No terms except an unconditional and immediate surrender can be accepted. I propose to move immediately on your works."

Buckner thought Grant's reply was "neither generous nor chivalrous," but the terms were accepted. The next day Buckner surrendered the fort and almost 15,000 men—the greatest number of prisoners in American military history up to this time.

When news of the fall of Fort Donelson reached Washington, Grant was an overnight hero. Bull Run had been avenged, and there was rejoicing throughout the North. People matched Grant's initials with his demand for *u*nconditional *s*urrender and he became "Unconditional Surrender" Grant. Interestingly, at West Point Grant had been called "Uncle

Sam" Grant because of his initials when actually his name was not Ulysses S. Grant but Hiram Ulysses Grant. An enrollment officer had made the mistake in writing down Grant's name and Grant had not wanted to go through the red tape of having it corrected. And anyway, Grant later said, "Who wants to be nicknamed HUG?"

Lincoln was, of course, overjoyed at the news. He immediately promoted Grant to major general, which made him outrank every officer in the western theater except Halleck. Halleck was, in fact, the only officer who did not rejoice over Grant's meteoric success, since he feared him as a rival. Halleck began to send tales back to McClellan in Washington that Grant had returned to drinking—which was untrue—and should be relieved of his command and put on the shelf. McClellan in turn relayed these stories to Lincoln, whose only comment was: "I cannot spare this man. He fights." When the stories continued, Lincoln suggested that McClellan find out what brand it was that Grant drank so that he could supply the same brand to the rest of the Northern generals.

Unperturbed, Grant simply began to prepare his army for its next attack. This proved to be the bloody battle of Shiloh, where some of the luster was rubbed off Grant's shiny image.

BLOODY SHILOH

Partly to pacify him, President Lincoln put Halleck in command of all of the Union's western armies on March 11, 1862. This put him in charge of four armies numbering more than 100,000 men. The four armies were Grant's Army of the Tennessee, Brigadier General Samuel Curtis' Army of the Southwest in Missouri and Arkansas, Brigadier General Don Carlos Buell's Army of the Ohio, and Major General John Pope's Army of the Mississippi.

Halleck's plan was to have Grant's army continue south up the Tennessee River to Pittsburg Landing. Nearby was a country meetinghouse built of rude logs known as Shiloh Church. Grant was to be supported by Buell's army, which Halleck also ordered up the Tennessee to Savannah. Savannah and Pittsburg Landing, both in Tennessee, were just nine miles apart. Curtis' army was also supposed to come to the support of Grant and Buell, but it was delayed by having to fight a battle with the Confederate forces at Pea Ridge, Arkansas. Curtis' troops defeated the Rebels under Major General Earl Van Dorn at Pea Ridge but were further delayed because of flooded rivers between them and the Shiloh battle area.

Confederate commander Albert Sidney Johnston was, of course, well aware of Grant's and Buell's troop movements. Johnston, with an army of 40,000 men, was just across the Tennessee-Mississippi border at Corinth, Mississippi. Nashville had fallen after the Union successes at Forts Henry and Donelson, and Johnston was fearful of a complete Confederate collapse in the western theater. To prevent this, Johnston planned to attack and defeat Grant in a direct frontal assault at Pittsburg Landing. He planned to do this before Buell could come to Grant's aid from Savannah.

Grant was not suspecting an attack. Mistakenly, he thought the morale of Johnston's troops was shattered. After Grant's 33,000 men went ashore at Pittsburg Landing they pitched tents in three lines of battle in front of and behind Shiloh Church, but they dug no entrenchments. In addition, they put out no cavalry scouting patrols; in fact, very little patroling of any kind was done. As a result, Johnston's army was able to march the twenty miles from Corinth and reach a wooded point just two miles from Grant's forces on the night of April 5–6 without being detected.

At dawn on the morning of April 6, the Confederates came charging out of the woods, guns blazing and Rebel yells filling the air. The surprised Yankees rolled out of their tents and attempted to stem the Rebel onrush right in the camp's company streets. The defense was spirited but futile. Many Union troops hastily retreated two miles to the northeast to Pittsburg Landing on the Tennessee River. By noon the Confederates had driven past Shiloh Church and were slowly but steadily driving forward all along the frontal assault line.

There was one pocket of Union resistance, however, that the Rebels could not reduce. This was in the center of the Yankee line of battle, where a division of Union troops under Brigadier General Benjamin Prentiss had fought a stubborn retreating action through a peach orchard in full bloom and finally dug in along a sunken road. From here they refused to retreat farther, and Prentiss' position with its continued hum of gunfire was immediately dubbed the Hornet's Nest by the Rebels. So thick was the small-arms fire around the Hornet's Nest that more than one soldier afterward claimed to have seen swarms of bullets in flight like masses of insects. Other soldiers hearing bullets patter among the leaves mistook the sound for falling rain. From the peach orchard more than sixty Rebel artillery pieces fired at the Hornet's Nest and a dozen infantry attacks stormed it to no avail.

Grant's headquarters were several miles away from the battle line when the fighting began. He had severely sprained his ankle a few days earlier when his horse had fallen, pinning him to the ground, but he now ignored the injury and hurried into the thick of the fight. On his way to the battle area Grant paused long enough to alert a Union detachment under Major General Lew Wallace and tell it to proceed to Shiloh. (Wallace was to be late in arriving at the battle and thus fail to gain the fame that was later to be his for writing *Ben Hur*.) Grant also ordered Buell's troops to hurry from Savannah.

When Grant arrived at the scene of the fighting, he found almost total chaos. Both the Yankee and Rebel troops were green and did not know how to cope with either victory or defeat. At Pittsburg Landing there was a crowd of Yankee battlefield deserters. Grant ignored these men, but he immediately established a stragglers' line to prevent any more Union troops from leaving their positions. In addition, he established an artillery unit on high ground to protect the landing area where Wallace's and Buell's troops were supposed to arrive.

On the battlefield itself both sides seemed to have lost control of the overall combat action, which had disintegrated into separate small fights among swarms of men. In many places high-ranking officers were leading squads of men numbering no more than a dozen or two. General Johnston himself led one of the numerous unsuccessful attacks on the Hornet's Nest. Later, he also rallied his reluctant men to make what proved to be a successful attack against the Yankees in the peach orchard that bloomed so brightly with both petals and the blood of wounded and dying men.

Noting his men's reluctance to continue through the murderous fire from the peach orchard, Johnston said it would have to be taken with the bayonet. "I will lead you!" he shouted.

When the Yanks had been driven from the orchard, Johnston rode back from the fighting, unhurt but with his uniform torn and one sole dangling from his boot where a bullet had ripped it loose.

"They failed to trip me up this time," Johnston said.

Moments later, an aide saw Johnston spin in his saddle as a bullet hit him.

"Are you hurt, sir?" the aide asked.

"Yes, and I fear seriously," Johnston said.

The aide helped Johnston from his saddle and saw that he had been shot in the leg and the wound was pumping blood. A tourniquet would undoubtedly have saved Johnston's life, but before someone was found who could apply one Johnston had bled to death. Johnston's death was an enormous loss to the South. "When he fell," Jefferson Davis said later, "I knew our strongest pillar was broken."

Beauregard now took command of the battle for the Confederacy, but the forward momentum of the fight was lost by the Rebels. Although Prentiss and his men had been overrun by the Rebels under Johnston in late afternoon, Grant succeeded in rallying his Union troops when their left flank was threatened. If this flank had collapsed, the entire Union army would have been trapped in a pocket between the Tennessee River and a tributary, Snake Creek.

Like Johnston, Grant rode into the midst of battle, bullets swarming around him, but he paid them no heed. At one point where the fire was especially severe an aide said to Grant, "General, we must leave this place. It isn't necessary to stay here. If we do, we'll all be dead in five minutes." Reluctantly Grant grumbled, "I guess that's so, but I do have to see just what's going on," and slowly moved to a more sheltered spot.

Grant's presence enormously cheered his troops, and his calm commands as he moved defensive units back into battle and prepared them for counterattack seemed to be unerring. After Grant arrived, the Union army's defense visibly stiffened.

In the late afternoon, Beauregard directed one final bayonet charge against Pittsburg Landing, but this was repulsed. Beauregard was completely out of reserve forces at this point, and many of his men were out of ammunition. There was nothing to do but call off the Confederate attack.

That night Wallace and his men, and Buell and some of his men, finally arrived at the battlefield. (Wallace had gotten lost, taking a wrong road to the area, and the long march from Savannah had delayed Buell.) With their arrival, Grant prepared to go on the offensive in the morning.

Beauregard was completely surprised by Grant's dawn attack around Shiloh Church on April 7. The Confederate general had already notified Jefferson Davis in Richmond of the great Southern victory of the day before, but now he realized that Grant did not know he had been beaten.

The second day's fighting was as bloody as the first, but with his reinforcements from Wallace and Buell, Grant would not be denied. Slowly, the Confederates began to fall back. Finally the slow withdrawal became a full retreat toward Corinth. Grant was tempted to follow them, but he knew his own army was completely exhausted. He also agreed with General Sherman, who had played a key role in both days' fighting and now commented, "We've had quite enough of their society for two whole days. I'm glad to be rid of them on any terms."

The terms came high. The two days proved to be the bloodiest of the war, the Union casualties coming to almost 14,000 men and the Confederate casualties to almost 11,000.

Halleck now let Grant take the brunt of the criticism for being surprised at the start of this battle and decided he would take whatever fame there was to gain from its result by personally leading the Union forces against Corinth. Not wanting to be surprised by any possible Rebel counterattack, Halleck made his troops dig entrenchments every night, and frequently they stayed in these entrenchments for several days at a time. Because of such overcautionary measures, it took Halleck and the combined Union armies a month to march the twenty miles to Corinth. When he got there, Beauregard and his army were gone.

Meanwhile, the North was gaining naval as well as army successes in the western theater of war during this period. Commodore Foote and his gunboats were active on the Mississippi River. Foote and infantry troops under General Pope captured New Madrid, Missouri, and an important Rebel fort on what was called Island Number Ten. Other gunboats also defeated a Confederate fleet at Memphis, which was soon abandoned by the Confederates. Vicksburg then became the main Rebel defense point on the Mississippi.

Even farther south, Union navy captain David Farragut with twenty-three steam sloops and wooden gunboats entered the Mississippi from the Gulf of Mexico. Farragut's small fleet was attacked by armored rams and fireboats and had to run a gantlet of fire from two Rebel forts, but succeeded in landing Union troops under Major General Benjamin Butler, who captured New Orleans by the end of April.

Aside from a Union victory at Perryville, Kentucky, in October and a Confederate-Union draw in which both sides claimed victory at Murfreesboro, Tennessee (a battle usually called Stones River), as the year ended, not much else was accomplished by the North or the South in the West during 1862.

The year had not been a good one for the Confederacy in the West, with the Union now threatening to take over the whole Mississippi Valley. In the East, however, the story was entirely different. There, by autumn, it looked like the Confederacy would win the war.

Admiral David Farragut. (LIBRARY OF CONGRESS)

McCLELLAN PLANS
A PENINSULAR
CAMPAIGN

President Lincoln felt great sorrow over the casualties that both sides suffered all during the war. Added to his sorrow was a great personal grief over the death of one of "Mrs. Lincoln's Zouaves" early in 1862. This was the president's son, young Willie Lincoln, who died in the White House in February.

Both Willie and his younger brother, Tad, had fallen ill with what was probably typhoid fever. During this illness, the two boys were often visited by one of their Zouave cadet playmates, young Bud Taft, son of Washington judge Horatio Taft.

Late one night the president found Bud by Willie's bedside. Lincoln patted both Willie and Bud and said quietly: "Bud, you should go home and get to bed."

"But if I go, he'll call for me," Bud said.

Later, Lincoln found Bud sound asleep and carried him off to bed in another White House room.

A few days later, on February 20, 1862, Bud was

holding Willie's hand when he died. Although Tad recovered, life for President and Mrs. Lincoln was never again the same.

Willie's funeral was attended by all of official Washington, including General in Chief McClellan, whose eyes were noticeably wet during the services. The boy's body was temporarily buried in a vault in Washington, where it would remain until one day it would accompany the body of his assassinated father on a funeral train back to a cemetery in their hometown of Springfield, Illinois.

A few days after Willie's funeral, General McClellan put his Army of the Potomac on the move toward Harpers Ferry. Having grown completely impatient with McClellan's "slows," President Lincoln had ordered an advance on Richmond by the end of February. Before attacking Richmond, however, McClellan wanted to move Union troops into the Shenandoah Valley. To get them there and to keep them supplied a new bridge had to be built across the Potomac at Harpers Ferry.

As the army moved out, boats were floated up a canal that led into the Potomac. These canal boats were intended to be used as bases on which the new pontoon bridge was to rest. Once the pontoon bridge was in place, both troops and supplies would be able to pour across it. But when the troops arrived and an attempt was made to float the boats through the locks from the canal to the Potomac, it was discovered that the boats were too wide to get through the locks.

McClellan and his embarrassed army had no

choice but to come tramping back to Washington.

Lincoln's comment on this fiasco was to observe that the expedition had apparently died of lockjaw.

But Lincoln was not really amused. On March 11 McClellan was relieved as general in chief of the Union armies but allowed to keep his command of the Army of the Potomac. Lincoln's face-saving reason for this move was to say that it would give Little Mac greater opportunity to concentrate on attacking Richmond. Temporarily, no one was named general in chief, Lincoln himself assuming many of these duties with the aid of Secretary of War Edwin M. Stanton.

Lincoln did not relieve McClellan of the overall Union command only because of the canal boat comedy of errors. The president was also irritated because Little Mac had not moved against General Joseph Johnston's Confederate troops when they reoccupied the old Bull Run battlefield. McClellan insisted that Johnston's army far outnumbered his, but later, when the Rebel troops pulled out to a better position along the Rappahannock River, it was discovered that just the reverse was true. In addition, Union troops found a number of wooden cannons that Johnston had used to bluff McClellan out of making an attack. When the public learned of this trick and how easily McClellan had been taken in by it, Little Mac's popularity fell and word began to go around Washington that McClellan might actually be a Southern sympathizer in disguise.

When McClellan at long last decided to make his

move against Richmond, he did not plan to advance overland because several rivers blocked the route between Washington and the Confederate capital. Instead he planned to move down Chesapeake Bay to Union-held Fort Monroe and then advance up the Virginia peninsula to attack Richmond. A Gibraltar-like stronghold, Fort Monroe was at the tip of the peninsula about eighty miles from Richmond.

Neither Lincoln nor Stanton objected to McClellan's plan, but both insisted that he leave enough troops behind to protect Washington. Stanton in particular went into a panic every time the Confederates made even a slight move toward the Federal capital, and he and Lincoln were both well aware of Stonewall Jackson's command roaming virtually at will up and down the nearby Shenandoah Valley. As a result, 40,000 men were taken from Little Mac's 130,000-man Army of the Potomac and placed under General McDowell to protect Washington. It was hoped McDowell would fare better than he had at Bull Run.

In making his plans to attack Richmond by way of the Virginia peninsula, McClellan assumed that the powerful Union navy would protect his flanks. The peninsula was bounded on the east by the York River and Chesapeake Bay, on the west by the James River, and on the south by Hampton Roads. The key to the success of McClellan's expedition was the control of these waters by the U.S. Navy.

But just as the Army of the Potomac was about to embark in its wooden transports that would carry it down Chesapeake Bay to Fort Monroe, some extremely disturbing news was received in Washington. Early in March a Confederate ironclad gunboat, the *Merrimack*, had defeated part of the Union navy at Hampton Roads just off Fort Monroe. The day after this action the *Merrimack* had fought another battle with a strange new Union ironclad called the *Monitor*. This fight had been a draw, but the *Merrimack* was still at large. McClellan had to ask himself, Could he land his large amphibious force at Fort Monroe in the face of deadly and destructive fire from the Confederate ironclad *Merrimack*?

THE MONITOR
AND THE
MERRIMACK

Originally, the *Merrimack* was a Union vessel. In fact, at the start of the war the Confederacy had no navy at all, and the Union had some ninety warships. Less than half of these were steam-driven—the navies of the world were just being converted from sail to steam—and five were powerful steam frigates. One of these was the *Merrimack,* a wooden vessel but heavily armed.

When the war began, the *Merrimack* was undergoing repairs to her engines at the Norfolk, Virginia, navy yard. The Confederates seized this yard on April 20, 1861, but before they could do so Federal sailors burned and sank all the Union ships. The *Merrimack* was only partially destroyed by fire, however, and Confederate engineers succeeded in recovering the scuttled hulk. They then set about not only repairing the damaged ship but also turning her into an unsinkable ironclad.

Stephen R. Mallory, secretary of the nonexistent Southern navy, had been dreaming of just such an unsinkable ship for some time. He now put Navy lieutenant John M. Brooke and civilian shipbuilder John L. Porter in charge of building her. The ship they constructed was like no other vessel that had been seen before. Her hull had been cut down to a point just above the water line. Her low, sloping roof was covered with sheet iron four inches thick. She also had a cast-iron prow that could be used to ram enemy vessels. And her armament consisted of ten heavy cannons. By the time she sailed forth to do battle on March 8, 1862, she had been renamed the *Virginia,* but she was rarely called anything but the *Merrimack.*

While the Confederate ironclad was being built, word of her construction leaked out to officers of the U.S. Navy Department. They knew that a Federal ironclad had to be built to combat the *Merrimack,* but it wasn't until the autumn of 1861 that construction of such a vessel began. In charge of designing and building her was a Swedish engineer living in the United States, John Ericsson. Ericsson's plan was so radical that the U.S. Navy made him agree to return the $300,000 it would cost to build the warship if she proved unsuccessful.

Ericsson named his "cheese box on a raft," as she was often called, the *Monitor* because, he said, it would admonish the Confederacy not to try to stop the Union naval and military advances. The *Monitor* was a small vessel with an ironclad deck just

Officers of the U.S.S. Monitor *grouped by the ship's turret.*
(LIBRARY OF CONGRESS, PHOTO BY J. F. GIBSON)

The battle between the Monitor *and the* Merrimack. (LIBRARY OF
CONGRESS)

The sinking Monitor *is abandoned as crewmen clamber down the turret to a boat from the U.S.S.* Rhode Island *in an engraving from* Harper's Weekly *of January 24, 1863, less than a month after the ironclad foundered in 220 feet of water during a gale 16 miles off Cape Hatteras.* (NATIONAL GEOGRAPHIC SOCIETY)

The ironclad U.S.S. Monitor *lies upside-down in this mosaic of undersea photos pieced together by navy technicians. The Civil War vessel was found by a National Geographic–Duke University team. Identifying features include: (1) distinctive anchor well at the bow; (2) armor belt around the hull; (3) the revolving gun turret, which slid off as the wreck sank and rests partly under the stern.* (© NATIONAL GEOGRAPHIC SOCIETY; PHOTOS BY GLEN TILLMAN, ALCOA MARINE CORP.; PHOTOMOSAIC BY U.S. NAVY)

a foot above the water line. The only visible feature on her deck was a pilothouse with a revolving gun turret that enabled the gun crew to aim and fire in any direction without the captain having to maneuver the ship. The turret housed two guns. Built in Brooklyn, New York, the *Monitor* was barely completed in time to combat the marauding *Merrimack.*

When the Confederate ironclad *Merrimack* came steaming out of the mouth of the Elizabeth River on a Saturday afternoon in early March, she sailed across Hampton Roads to Newport News and immediately attacked two Union warships, the *Cumberland* and the *Congress.* Despite heavy fire from the warships' seventy-five guns as well as from several Union shore batteries, the *Merrimack* rammed and sank the *Cumberland.* The *Congress,* trying to escape, was run ashore, where she later burned and exploded. Other Union ships now hurried from Fort Monroe, but fire from their guns had no more effect on the *Merrimack* "than peas from a popgun." Almost casually, the Confederate ironclad steamed out of range as the day ended, leaving behind her complete chaos in the Union fleet and 250 Union dead. Her own casualties were few, but among them was the *Merrimack*'s commander, Captain Franklin Buchanan, who was wounded. As the day's fighting ended, the *Monitor* arrived on the scene, having almost sunk in the heavy seas. Most of her crew were seasick or ill from gases that had collected below-decks when water swamped her ventilators. But by dawn of the next day, March 9, 1862, the Union sailors had recovered and were ready for the duel between the *Monitor* and the *Merrimack.*

Crowds lined the shores of Hampton Roads on the day of what promised to be one of history's great naval battles. What they saw was exciting but inconclusive. The new commander of the *Merrimack* was Lieutenant Catesby Jones. The *Monitor* was commanded by Lieutenant John L. Worden. As the two ships moved into action, it immediately was apparent that the smaller *Monitor* was also much faster and more maneuverable than the *Merrimack.* When the *Merrimack* tried to ram the *Monitor,* the Union vessel quickly dodged out of the way. The guns from neither vessel had any effect on the ironclad deck of her opponent, but in one exchange a bursting shell blinded *Monitor* commander Worden, who was replaced by Lieutenant Samuel D. Greene.

At the end of four hours of fighting the battle was a draw, neither ship being able to gain success over the other. But a draw was almost as good as a victory for the North. The *Merrimack* retreated back up the Elizabeth River, and the *Monitor* remained on guard in Hampton Roads. What the North now feared, however, was the possible future destruction of the *Monitor.* If this happened, the entire Union navy might still be destroyed by the *Merrimack.* President Lincoln had word passed to Lieutenant Greene to take extra care before engaging in any future combat action.

During the next several weeks the *Merrimack* underwent repairs at the Norfolk navy yard, including the installation of a new iron prow. While the Confederate ironclad was in dry dock, McClellan's Army of the Potomac began its embarkation and amphibious movement toward Fort Monroe on March 17.

Early in April the *Merrimack* reappeared in Hampton Roads, but returned to Norfolk after firing a single harmless broadside at the *Monitor*. From this date on there developed something of a naval stalemate in Hampton Roads, the *Merrimack* occasionally threatening to break out into Chesapeake Bay, where it could cause further damage to Union shipping and perhaps attack Washington, and the *Monitor* and other U.S. Navy vessels remaining on duty to prevent such a breakout. This stalemate further handicapped McClellan in waging his peninsular campaign.

Eventually, however, the *Merrimack*'s base at Norfolk was captured by Union troops, and to prevent the capture of the courageous Confederate ironclad it was blown up and destroyed off Craney Island at the mouth of the Elizabeth River on May 11, 1862.

The *Monitor* met an equally sad fate, sinking in a storm off Cape Hatteras on December 31, 1862. Thus the two opponents in the world's first battle of the ironclads found similar watery graves. They had caused a revolution in sea warfare, however, for in the future wooden ships and the iron men who fought in them would gradually be replaced by iron and steel ships with equally courageous if somewhat more sophisticated crews.

Interestingly, the remains of the *Monitor* were discovered more than a century later, on August 27, 1973, by a National Geographic–Duke University team led by scientist John G. Newton aboard the research ship *Eastward*. Through the use of sonar detection devices for scanning the ocean floor and an underwater television camera, the wreck of the *Monitor* was found and photographed on tape. Later, more than 2,000 separate underwater photographs were taken, positively identifying the lost ironclad. The remains were so badly corroded and fragile, however, that scientists agreed the ship could not be raised intact. Nevertheless, the site where the *Monitor* sank some sixteen miles off Cape Hatteras was made a National Marine Sanctuary in January 1975.

McCLELLAN'S PENINSULAR CAMPAIGN

McClellan's army of 90,000 men was safely landed at Fort Monroe and Newport News by April 1, 1862. Among those landing at Fort Monroe was a civilian, Mathew B. Brady, whose photographic coverage of this campaign as well as much of the rest of the war was to make him world-famous. Brady paid all his own expenses to make his priceless photographic record of the war.

McClellan immediately moved his army toward Yorktown, the site of George Washington's great victory over the British in the American Revolution.* This time, however, one of the opposition's actors was to play the key role in a month-long defensive drama. This was Confederate Major General John B. Magruder, a well-known amateur actor who

*See another book in this series, *The American Revolution, America's First War for Independence.*

Dollar-a-pound cotton used for Confederate fortifications at Yorktown. (LIBRARY OF CONGRESS)

now skillfully used all his dramatic talents to fool McClellan.

Magruder had only 15,000 men to defend York-town. But as soon as McClellan's forces approached, Magruder ordered his men to parade back and forth in plain view but out of gunfire range. This constant troop movement at all hours of the day, plus inaccurate reports from civilian detectives acting as Union intelligence agents, convinced McClellan that he was badly outnumbered by the Confederates. In addition, McClellan was getting little or no naval support in the rivers on his flanks because the Union navy was concentrated in Hampton Roads to neutralize any threatened attack by the *Merrimack*. Consequently, McClellan decided to lay siege to Yorktown. Many useless days and weeks were spent in erecting fortifications to house mortars and siege guns when one quick thrust would have defeated the Confederates.

Meanwhile, Stonewall Jackson in the Shenandoah Valley was firmly establishing his reputation as one of the best combat commanders not only in the Confederate army but in the Union army as well. Well aware of Lincoln's sensitivity about any threat to Washington, Jackson decided on a classic campaign of rapid maneuver that would pin down Union forces in the Shenandoah Valley which might otherwise be sent to support McClellan.

Jackson's forces numbered just 17,000 men. Yet by keeping them constantly on the move, making a slashing surprise night attack here, disappearing into the darkness and making another bold dawn raid there, Jackson succeeded in virtually immobilizing Union forces of more than 50,000 men. In several lightning-like trips up and down the Shenandoah Valley between the end of March and the first week in June, Jackson fought half a dozen battles against the bewildered forces of Union generals Irvin McDowell, Nathaniel P. Banks, and John C. Frémont, winning all but one. He then swept out of the Shenandoah Valley and moved down to Richmond, which by then was being threatened by McClellan's Army of the Potomac.

McClellan did not move against Yorktown until May 5. By then the Confederate defenders had been reinforced by some 65,000 men under the Bull Run victor, General Joseph Johnston. But Johnston did not want to do battle with McClellan before Yorktown. He preferred a spot closer to the Confederate capital. Consequently, Johnston pulled all his troops out of Yorktown on May 3, so that when the Yankees stormed the Yorktown defenses they found no Rebels there.

Johnston retreated slowly up the peninsula toward Richmond, his rear covered by Brigadeer General Jeb Stuart's cavalry and Major General James Longstreet's infantry. McClellan's advance cavalry caught up with Johnston's rear guard at Williamsburg late in the day on May 5 but was driven off by Longstreet. The retreat and leisurely pursuit continued until May 25, when the Confederates reached Richmond and the Union army went into camp on swampy ground on both sides of the Chickahominy River. Here McClellan expected to be joined by General McDowell's forces, but they were delayed by Stonewall Jackson in the Shenandoah Valley.

Richmond was just six miles from McClellan's army straddled across the Chickahominy. The city's church spires could be seen and the church bells could be heard by men in the Yankee camp, and a Union observer, Thaddeus Lowe, sent aloft in a balloon—this was one of the first uses of a balloon in warfare for observation purposes—reported not only on the activity of Rebel troops but also on the comings and goings of civilians walking the streets of the Confederate capital.

As the two sides prepared for battle, Yankee and Rebel soldiers in advance outpost positions frequently visited with one another, exchanging gossip, newspapers, and food. This brief bit of fraternization was abruptly brought to an end when the Confederates struck the Union army south of the Chickahominy at Fair Oaks (also called Seven Pines) on May 31. Results of the battle were inconclusive, but the Confederates lost one of their top generals when Joe Johnston was wounded in the fighting. He was replaced by the greatest general the South was to produce, Robert E. Lee, who would command the Confederacy's most famous fighting force, the Army of Northern Virginia.

Lee's star had been somewhat in eclipse up to this time. Son of the Revolutionary War hero, Light-

Thaddeus Lowe ascends in his balloon Intrepid *to observe Confederate forces in the Peninsular Campaign.* (LIBRARY OF CONGRESS)

horse Harry Lee, Robert E. Lee had distinguished himself in combat in both the Mexican War and in battle against the Indians along the Texas border. Since the start of the Civil War, however, he had been serving as military adviser to Jefferson Davis and was a general without an army of his own. But as the new commander of the Army of Northern Virginia, Lee's great military career was about to begin. A natural field commander, Lee was daring, aggressive, and a brilliant strategist. He was also a leader to whom his fellow officers and soldiers were totally devoted.

Lee always rode a huge gray horse called Traveller. He had bought Traveller as a colt for $200 from a young Confederate captain named Broun after Broun had offered to give him to Lee. Lee and Traveller soon became twin symbols of the Confederacy, and both were greatly loved by the men who followed the gallant horse and rider into battle after battle. Lee rode Traveller not only throughout the war but also during the years afterward when Lee became president of Washington (later Washington and Lee) College. When Lee died in 1870, Traveller —his saddle empty—walked behind the hearse bearing his master's body in the funeral procession. Two years later Traveller also died. His skeleton was later mounted and put on display at Washington and Lee, where his master was also buried.

Lee had no intention of letting his army conduct a siege defense at Richmond. He planned to strike McClellan before Little Mac could launch an attack

General Robert E. Lee. (U.S. SIGNAL CORPS PHOTO, NATIONAL ARCHIVES, BRADY COLLECTION)

of his own. To do so, however, Lee had to know exactly where McClellan's troops were located. To get this information Lee sent Jeb Stuart and 1,200 Confederate cavalrymen on a hard-riding reconnaissance mission that circled completely around the Army of the Potomac. Covering 150 miles in three days, Stuart reported back to Richmond that McClellan's weakest spot was the right flank of his army north of the Chickahominy. Immediately Lee ordered Stonewall Jackson, who had just arrived from the Shenandoah Valley, to join with Lee's main army and smash McClellan's right flank. The result was the Seven Days' Battles, which began on June 25, 1862.

The Seven Days' Battles were fought at Oak Grove, Mechanicsville, Gaines' Mill (Cold Harbor), Savage's Station, Frayser's Farm, and Malvern Hill. Their overall result was a series of bloody Confederate advances at the end of which McClellan's Army of the Potomac retreated to the James River, where he hoped that now that the *Merrimack* had been destroyed Union gunboats would give him badly needed support from their heavy guns to prevent a complete Union rout. The bloodiest fighting of all occurred at Malvern Hill on the James River on July 1, where Lee was convinced that one final thrust would drive Little Mac's army into the river. Here the Union army stood its ground and, aided by massed artillery fire, cut down some 5,000 advancing Rebels and caused the rest of Lee's army to leave the field of battle and return to Richmond.

General J. E. B. "Jeb" Stuart. (U.S. SIGNAL CORPS PHOTO, NATIONAL ARCHIVES, BRADY COLLECTION)

McClellan then retreated to a new base at Harrison's Landing farther down the James River. Here his men dug in while McClellan began to bombard Washington with requests for reinforcements so he could renew his campaign. But at this point the Union War Department was having serious doubts about McClellan himself as well as about any further attempts to capture Richmond by frontal assault. Instead, it was suggested by Secretary of War Stanton, the Army of the Potomac should probably be brought back to northern Virginia. President Lincoln decided to go to McClellan's headquarters to determine the matter for himself.

After visiting with McClellan—during the course of their visit Little Mac played a true Young Napoleon role by giving Lincoln a long letter telling the president just how the entire war should be conducted—Lincoln decided that the Army of the Potomac should return to its Washington base.

The Peninsular Campaign had been a failure for the North and enormously costly to both sides in dead and wounded. The Union suffered almost 16,000 total casualties, and the Confederacy, which had done most of the attacking, more than 20,000. From these fearful losses grew perhaps just one positive result. This was the composition of "Taps," the most haunting of all military bugle calls.

After the Seven Days' Battles, while the Union army was bivouacked at Harrison's Landing, Brigadeer General Daniel A. Butterfield was filled with a feeling of great sadness over the loss of so many of his young men in the 3rd Union Brigade, which he commanded. Hearing the traditional army call, "Extinguish Lights," each evening, Butterfield did not think it suited the occasion. A brief, more haunting melody kept running through his mind, and he had an aide write down the notes. On the night before the Fourth of July, Butterfield had his bugler, twenty-two-year-old Oliver W. Norton, play the new Taps, which was an instant success. The next day buglers throughout the Army of the Potomac besieged Norton for copies of the music, which he supplied. Within a matter of months the new Taps had replaced the old Extinguish Lights throughout the Union army, and Confederate buglers also took up the tune. In fact, Taps was sounded over Stonewall Jackson's grave when that heroic Southern general lost his life in battle less than a year later. Taps was officially adopted by the United States in 1874.

TURNING POINT
OF THE WAR

In July of 1862 President Lincoln decided against continuing to act as his own general in chief of the Union armies and recalled General Halleck from the West to take over that post. Serious consideration was also given to removing General McClellan from command of the Army of the Potomac, but instead McClellan remained in charge while his army was fed in bits and pieces to General John Pope.

Pope, like Halleck, had been recalled from the West, where his Army of the Mississippi had been successful in the capture of Island Number Ten and other key Confederate strongholds in the Mississippi Valley. He was now put in charge of the North's newly created Army of Virginia, which Lincoln hoped would drive the Rebels from the Shenandoah Valley and relieve the threat against Washington.

General Lee had very little respect for Pope,

General Henry Halleck. (LIBRARY OF CONGRESS)

88

whom he had known before the war. Lee regarded him as a comic braggart who talked a good fight but was short on delivering results. Pope did indeed brag about being a man of action, a general whose headquarters were in the saddle. On this Lee commented that Pope's headquarters were where his hindquarters ought to be.

Partially out of a lack of respect for Pope but mainly because of his own great daring and masterful sense of timing, Lee decided to break a cardinal military rule in fighting Pope: He would divide his forces in the face of the enemy. First of all, Lee knew that if he waited for all of McClellan's forces to join Pope's army, the Confederates would be overwhelmingly outnumbered. Immediately he ordered Stonewall Jackson and 25,000 men to circle around the right side of Pope's 75,000-man army and cut off Pope's supply and communications route to Washington. Jackson's men accomplished this feat in two days, falling on Pope's supply base at Manassas Junction, capturing and destroying all of the Federal supplies there, and tearing up the railroad tracks. When Pope arrived on the scene, the Rebels were gone, having taken up a strong defensive position at Stony Ridge. This was near the scene of the First Battle of Bull Run, where Jackson had first won his nickname.

Meanwhile, Lee had sent other powerful forces against Pope's left flank. These were led by Major General James Longstreet. With 30,000 men, Longstreet went into position alongside Jackson on August 29. Here Pope ignored Longstreet and centered his attack on Jackson at Stony Ridge, giving the unengaged Longstreet a perfect opportunity to smash the Yankee left. However, Longstreet, like his Union counterpart McClellan, also had the "slows" and failed to take advantage of the opportunity. Consequently, Jackson had to fight desperately to fend off the concentrated Federal attack. Convinced that he had won the battle and put Jackson on the run, Pope sent a victory message to Washington.

But the next day told a different story. Pope continued to advance against the slowly retreating Jackson, but this time Lee personally ordered Longstreet to attack Pope's left flank and the results were devastating. The Yankees in this Second Battle of Bull Run, or Second Manassas, just as in the first one were driven into full retreat. Now, however, the Union army had become a more professional one and the retreat was orderly.

One further battle was fought in the Second Bull Run campaign. This was at Chantilly on September 1, 1862. This engagement was indecisive, but in it the North's colorful one-armed general Philip Kearny was killed by Rebel riflemen as he galloped his horse through a Confederate outpost on a wild, storm-tossed late afternoon. Lee later returned Kearny's body to the Union army under a flag of truce.

This was the high point of the war for the Confederacy. Union forces had now been driven from virtually the whole of Virginia, and President Lin-

General John Pope's railway line before the Second Battle of Manassas. (NATIONAL ARCHIVES, GIFT COLLECTION)

Union railway lines destroyed by Confederates in Virginia. (LIBRARY OF CONGRESS)

coln was still trying to find a field commander who could lead the Army of the Potomac to victory. After Second Bull Run, Pope's and McClellan's forces were completely combined under the Army of the Potomac banner with McClellan once again in complete command. Although Little Mac had never literally been removed as commander, his authority had been bled away along with his combat divisions and Secretary of War Stanton was in favor of keeping it that way. But Lincoln, wise in judging men's emotional reactions, knew that Little Mac's men loved him still and that he was the only man who could once again restore their belief in themselves as soldiers.

In this Lincoln was right. Almost at once a joyous shout went up throughout the Army of the Potomac: "Little Mac is back!" And once again Little Mac rode among them on his big black horse, like a conquering hero rather than a general who had yet to achieve a major victory.

Within a few short weeks McClellan had breathed new life into the Army of the Potomac, and 100,000-strong it marched out of Washington to do battle with Lee's 60,000-man Army of Northern Virginia. The two great opposing forces were soon to meet in a battle that would be the turning point of the war on the dark and bloody ground near a town called Sharpsburg and a creek called the Antietam in the state of Maryland.

At this point in the war the South changed its overall strategy from defensive to offensive and decided to invade the North. The decision was made for both political and military reasons. First of all, both Confederate president Davis and General Lee thought that Northern public opinion in favor of peace would be strengthened by a Southern invasion. There were indeed a number of Northern Democrats who favored a negotiated peace, but Davis and Lee seriously misjudged the strength of these so-called Copperheads. (The term first appeared in the New York *Tribune* on July 21, 1861, and came from the poisonous snake of the same name.) The two Southern leaders also misjudged public opinion in Maryland, which they thought might secede and join the Confederacy if it were invaded.

But perhaps most important of all, Davis and Lee hoped that an invasion of the North would bring about recognition of the Confederate States of America as a legitimate independent nation by both France and Great Britain. Despite continued Southern military success in the eastern theater of war all through the spring and summer of 1862, the Union's blockade of the Confederate coastline had remained unbroken and was threatening to strangle the South. If France and Great Britain could be encouraged to enter the war on the side of the South, the great French and British war fleets could smash this blockade. So Davis and Lee decided to change Southern strategy and invade the North. If the invasion was successful, not only would the Army of the Potomac be destroyed, but the key cities of Washington, Baltimore, and Philadelphia would also fall and the North would lose the war.

A young "powder monkey." The first part of President Lincoln's comment that the war "robbed both the cradle and the grave" is aptly illustrated by this picture of a young crew member of the Union blockade ship New Hampshire. *Powder monkeys carried gunpowder from the magazines to the gun crews during naval engagements off the Confederate coasts.* (LIBRARY OF CONGRESS, BRADY COLLECTION)

After the Battle of Chantilly, Lee moved most of his army north across both the Potomac and the Blue Ridge Mountains at a point called Stone Mountain. However, he sent Stonewall Jackson's command against the Union garrison at Harpers Ferry. Lee had thus again divided his forces in the face of the enemy, but this time he was not to be so fortunate in his daring.

In mid-September, McClellan also moved toward Maryland with his Army of the Potomac. Along the way Little Mac experienced a stroke of unbelievably good luck. On September 13 he was given copies of Lee's battle plans for the entire Maryland campaign. These orders had been sent to one of Jackson's subordinates but a messenger had lost them. They had been found by two Union enlisted men and rushed by their officers to Little Mac. McClellan now had a matchless opportunity to defeat Lee's divided army if he quickly moved his army through the Blue Ridge Mountains at Turner's and Crampton gaps before Jackson could join Lee. But once again McClellan let a golden opportunity slip from his grasp when he failed to react with lightning speed. By the time McClellan's forces had made a leisurely passage through the Stone Mountain gaps, Stonewall Jackson had already taken Harpers Ferry and was driving hard to join Lee.

Once through the mountains, McClellan again delayed his attack on Lee, fearing—as usual—that the Yankee forces were badly outnumbered by the Rebels. Actually the Rebels were outnumbered almost two to one.

A scout (foreground) observes the actual battle scene at Antietam.
(LIBRARY OF CONGRESS)

A Union Field hospital. Confederate wounded were cared for here by medical officers of the Indiana Volunteers after the Battle of Antietam. (LIBRARY OF CONGRESS, PHOTO BY ALEXANDER GARDNER)

Lee decided to make his stand at Sharpsburg on Antietam Creek. This seemed a bold, if not foolhardy, decision since it pinned his army between the creek and the Potomac River and gave him little room in which to maneuver.

McClellan began a series of rapid but uncoordinated assaults against Lee on the misty morning of September 17. If these separate assaults had been carefully planned to coordinate with one another, or if indeed there had been one major assault, Lee's army would probably have been overwhelmed. At one point, in fact, the Confederate main line of defense was all but shattered, but McClellan refused to commit his final reserves, holding them out of action until he was certain Stonewall Jackson's entire army had arrived to support Lee. When the last of Jackson's men did arrive, they did so just in time to stave off McClellan's final attack.

When the brutal day's fighting ended, both armies occupied about the same ground they had occupied when the battle began. But there were far fewer men to occupy that ground. Of the 70,000 combat men in McClellan's attacking army, some 13,000 were killed, wounded, or missing. The 40,000-man Confederate combat army had suffered 8,000 casualties. This was the war's single most bloody day.

Although the battle seemed actually to be a standoff, Lee withdrew from the field and moved back into Virginia the following day. McClellan made no effort at pursuit.

President Lincoln meets with General McClellan and his staff.
(LIBRARY OF CONGRESS, PHOTO BY ALEXANDER GARDNER)

President Lincoln and General McClellan meet in the general's tent.
(LIBRARY OF CONGRESS, PHOTO BY ALEXANDER GARDNER)

99

Seizing upon Lee's withdrawal as a strategic victory, President Lincoln issued his famous Emancipation Proclamation on September 22. This proclamation declared that "all slaves in states or districts in rebellion against the United States on January 1, 1863, will be thenceforward and forever free."

Lincoln's move was a bold and ingenious one, having as much propaganda value as anything else. Up to this point the war had not been explicitly fought to free the slaves. Now "freeing the slaves" was the war's main Northern aim. Not only did it give the weight of a moral crusade to the Northern cause, but it also successfully kept foreign powers such as France and Britain from even considering throwing in their lot with the Confederacy, because to do so would mean they were fighting in *favor* of slavery.

Britain had almost entered the war in the autumn of 1861, when Captain Charles Wilkes and his United States ship *San Jacinto* stopped and boarded a British ship, the *Trent,* and seized two Europebound Confederate diplomats, James Mason and John Slidell. Similar action in reverse—by the British against the United States—had been a key cause of the War of 1812. This time apologies were made, the diplomats were released, and the so-called *Trent* Affair blew over.*

The Emancipation Proclamation actually did not immediately set free any slaves. But from the day it

*See another book in this series, *The United States in the War of 1812.*

Company E, 4th U.S. Infantry, founded during the war. (LIBRARY OF CONGRESS, PHOTO BY WILLIAM M. SMITH)

was issued, black persons throughout the land took new hope that eventually they would be free.

Soon after Antietam, General McClellan's military career ended. Lincoln relieved him as commander of the Army of the Potomac on November 7, 1862. In his place Lincoln named Major General Ambrose E. Burnside, whose greatest claim to fame proved to be his interesting side-whiskers that were trimmed in a unique fashion that came to be called "Burnsides" and thus eventually "sideburns."

Burnside was far from eager to accept the seemingly jinxed Potomac command, but good soldier that he was he took on the role and set about his new job with a will.

Burnside and Lee met in their first engagement at Fredericksburg, Virginia, on December 13, and the battle resulted in a costly Union defeat. From a strong defensive position on the high bluffs along the Rappahannock River, Lee's 78,000-man army repulsed six assaults by Burnside's 120,000 Yankees. In three days of fighting the Union lost 12,653 men and the Confederacy 5,309. Several days later Burnside was relieved of his command and replaced by Major General Joseph "Fighting Joe" Hooker.

At the end of 1862 gloom in the North over the failures in the eastern theater of war was almost unrelieved. But news from the western theater continued to be good. And it was from the West that the military leader for whom President Lincoln had been searching would finally come.

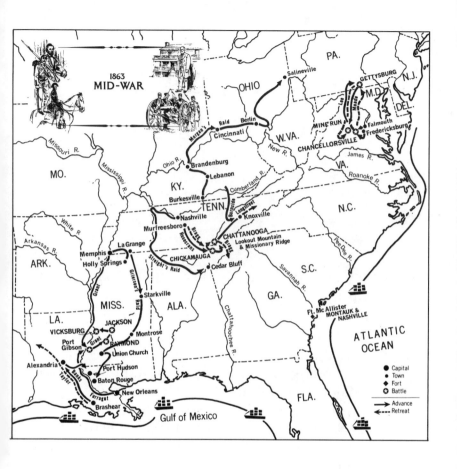

1863
MID-WAR

OHIO

PA.

Salineville

W.VA.

N.J.

GETTYSBURG

M.D.

DEL.

Morgan's Raid

Berlin

Cincinnati

MINE RUN

Meade

Falmouth

New R.

CHANCELLORSVILLE

Fredericksburg

Lee

Missouri R.

Mississippi R.

Ohio R.

Brandenburg

Lebanon

James R.

MO.

KY.

Cumberland R.

VA.

Roanoke R.

Burkesville

White R.

TENN.

Knoxville

N.C.

Nashville

Burnside

Murfreesboro

Longstreet

CHATTANOOGA

Arkansas R.

La Grange

Rosecrans

Bragg

Lookout Mountain
& Missionary Ridge

ARK.

Memphis

CHICKAMAUGA

Pee Dee R.

Holly Springs

Straight's Raid

Cedar Bluff

S.C.

Savannah R.

Starkville

Grant

Grierson's Raid

MISS.

ALA.

GA.

Chattahoochee R.

Ft. McAllister
MONTAUK &
NASHVILLE

LA.

JACKSON

VICKSBURG

Montrose

ATLANTIC
OCEAN

Port
Gibson

Grant

RAYMOND

Union Church

Alexandria

Banks

Port Hudson

Taylor

Baton Rouge

FLA.

Farragut

New Orleans

Brashear

Gulf of Mexico

● Capital
• Town
◆ Fort
✪ Battle

→ Advance
⇢ Retreat

GRANT TAKES VICKSBURG

The Vicksburg campaign began badly. First of all, Grant had to fight a determined rear-guard action by one of his own generals. This was more a political action than it was military, but it was nonetheless vital to the outcome of the war.

The rear-guard action against Grant was started by Major General John A. McClernand, a well-known Illinois politician who had fought at Shiloh. After Shiloh, McClernand had taken a leave of absence and gone to Washington to visit Lincoln and Stanton. He told them that he could recruit another army in the Middle West and that with this army he could sail down the Mississippi and take Vicksburg. Lincoln and Stanton liked the plan and told McClernand to go ahead with it. The only trouble was that nobody, not even General in Chief Halleck, told Grant about it.

When news of the supposedly top secret McClernand scheme began to leak out, Grant was understandably concerned about his own overall authority in the Mississippi area, especially in view of the fact that he and General Sherman were themselves mounting a campaign against Vicksburg. It took Grant many months to straighten out this effort at double-dealing and to reassert complete control over all the western operations. One of the ways he did so was simply to take charge of all the new troops that McClernand had enlisted in Illinois and then shipped to Grant's military department. Grant turned these troops over to Sherman and told him to get moving against Vicksburg. Thus, when McClernand himself finally arrived in the theater, he had no new army to command. He was, however, put in charge of one army corps under Grant in the actual Vicksburg campaign. In all these moves Grant was secretly supported by Halleck, who had no faith in McClernand as a top military leader, whereas his faith in Grant was growing stronger every day. Halleck, however, did not tell Grant about McClernand's plan because he did not want to appear to be disloyal to Lincoln and Stanton.

Grant next had to deal with another rear-guard action, but this was strictly military. It was led by a wild genius of a Confederate cavalry commander, Brigadier General Nathan Bedford Forrest, whose simple yet completely effective combat philosophy was "to git there fustest with the mostest." Grant's army was in northern Mississippi at this time, and his supply base was at Columbus, Kentucky. On a hard-riding raid Forrest and 2,500 troopers destroyed much of the railroad between Grant and his supply base, defeating several Union cavalry detachments along the way. This raid plus another led by Confederate major general Earl Van Dorn, in which a second major Federal supply base was destroyed at Holly Springs, Mississippi, seriously delayed Grant's campaign. It also kept him out of communication with Sherman, who with 30,000 men had moved down the Mississippi from Memphis and was advancing on Vicksburg, where Grant had planned to reinforce him. As a result, Sherman suffered a sharp defeat by Lieutenant General John Pemberton's Rebels in the Battle of Chickasaw Bluffs, Mississippi, and Grant had to revise his plans.

At the end of January 1863 Grant decided to abandon an overland attack on Vicksburg and to take personal charge of a Mississippi River expedition against the city. To do so he also planned to use his entire army of 45,000 men, which was divided into three corps under McClernand, Sherman, and Major General James B. McPherson. Later Grant received reinforcements that brought his strength to 75,000 men. He would need every man jack of them, for Vicksburg was to be a tough nut to crack.

Vicksburg was located at an almost ideal defensive site. High bluffs some 250 feet above the Mississippi ran along the river's eastern bank for almost 100 miles. Vicksburg was atop these. North and south of the city was swampy land that was almost impassable. The bluffs themselves, which ran north and south, had been heavily fortified from Haynes' Bluff on the Yazoo River about ten miles north of Vicksburg to Grand Gulf at the mouth of the Big Black River some forty miles south of the city. Sailing a fleet of warships and troopships downriver past these fortifications, and especially the fortifications at Vicksburg itself, would be extremely hazardous. The only likely place of attack seemed to be to the east of the city where the ground was high and dry. But to get there Grant's army would have to cross from the western bank of the Mississippi, where it was now stationed, to the eastern bank and then make its way around the city so it could attack it from the east. And then it would be caught between Pemberton's 30,000-man force of Vicksburg defenders and a somewhat smaller force of Rebels under General Joseph Johnston, who were located at Jackson, Mississippi, forty miles farther east of Vicksburg.

Grant tried a number of plans before he hit on a successful one. First of all he tried to change the course of the Mississippi! In the late winter and early spring of 1863 he set his army to work digging canals in the swampy land around Vicksburg. Opposite the city was a large peninsula formed by a huge U-bend in the river. Grant and his engineers thought that if a canal was dug through the base of this peninsula, the great river would flow out of its main channel and through this canal, leaving Vicksburg even higher and drier than it was. But once the canal was dug the great Father of Waters resolutely refused to change its course. Other canals were then dug above the city in an attempt to clear a way for troops to be transported to a disembarkation point near the high ground east of the river, but these, too, ended in failure.

Up to this time Grant's efforts had been mainly centered on trying to find access to Vicksburg from a point above or north of the city. In March he finally decided to abandon attempts at this approach and concentrate on some way of getting at the city by a southern approach. But to do this he would somehow have to transport his army down the Mississippi past the powerful guns at the fortress city, and he would therefore need aid from Rear Admiral David Porter and his naval forces.

Porter told Grant it would not be an impossible job to carry troops and supplies downriver past Vicksburg, but he pointed out that to do so would mean a total commitment to the plan. There could be no turning back, Porter explained, because his boats' engines simply were not powerful enough to move loaded transports back upstream against the powerful Mississippi current.

Grant consulted with Sherman regarding this plan and Sherman was flatly against it. He wanted to return the entire army to Memphis and start another overland attack. But Grant was firm. To return to Memphis would mean a retreat and an unacceptable defeat in the eyes of the Northern public. Grant decided to commit everything to this one move. If he won, the Union would control the entire Missis-

Admiral David Porter. (LIBRARY OF CONGRESS)

sippi River and the Confederacy would be hopelessly divided. If he lost, the blow might lose the war for the North.

The new plan for the Vicksburg campaign was carried out in a somewhat modified form. To keep both Pemberton and Johnston confused about Grant's intentions, Sherman's corps crossed the river above Vicksburg, pretended they were about to attack the city, and then returned to the west bank. In addition, Grant stole a page from the Confederate cavalry rule book and ordered a cavalry raid against the Rebels similar to Nathan Bedford Forrest's earlier raid against the Yankees. This raid was led by Colonel Benjamin H. Grierson, whose bold Union cavalry came charging through Confederate-held territory, tearing up railroads, slashing away at Rebel troops who tried to stop them, and thoroughly confusing both Pemberton and Johnston regarding Union plans.

Meanwhile, McClernand's and McPherson's corps did not sail but instead marched southward along the river's western bank while Porter led his fleet of empty transports, supply ships, and gunboats down the river past the powerful Vicksburg guns. All but one of Porter's ships ran the gantlet successfully. On April 30 Porter's little river navy began to ferry Grant's army across the river below Vicksburg at Bruinsburg. This move was also made successfully, as was that of Sherman's corps which followed just one week later.

Once the river crossing was made, Grant felt no

fear of the battles to come. Instead he felt only great relief because, as he later wrote, "I was on dry ground on the same side of the river with the enemy." As far as he was concerned his real worries were now over! His lack of concern was demonstrated when Sherman told him they should delay the attack on Vicksburg until their supply line was firmly established. Grant told him they couldn't wait, that speed was all-important.

"But what will we do for supplies?" Sherman asked.

"Live off the land," Grant said. And this they did, foraging through the countryside as they advanced. Consequently, at one point in the campaign, Pemberton wasted a major force of Confederate troops when he sent them to Grant's rear to cut off the nonexistent Yankee supply line.

Interestingly, one of Grant's "staff members" accompanying him on much of this campaign was his twelve-year-old son, Frederick. Fred and Grant's wife, Julia, had been visiting Grant at his headquarters for several weeks before the campaign began. When Mrs. Grant returned home, Fred insisted that he be allowed to stay with his father. Julia consented as long as the boy was kept safely away from any threat of combat. Grant agreed, and Fred's presence, the general later wrote, "caused no anxiety to me or to his mother."

But keeping young Fred away from the action was no simple problem. When Grant's troops began to cross the Mississippi, Fred was left in bed at the

111

army's rear headquarters in Bruinsburg. When he awakened, Fred attached himself to Charles A. Dana, a War Department observer assigned to Grant's headquarters, and accompanied him across the river to find Grant. Along the way Fred and Dana acquired a pair of ancient plow horses, which they rode right into Grant's advanced headquarters at Port Gibson. Fred, with Dana as his guardian, was allowed to remain with Grant's army for the rest of the campaign. Dressed in his father's formal parade-ground sash and commanding general's sword—fancy attire that Grant never used—Fred was regarded as something of a good-luck mascot by all of the men in Grant's command.

Still uncertain about Grant's plans, Pemberton had dispersed his troops to points at Vicksburg, along the Big Black River, and along the route between Vicksburg and Jackson, where Johnston was hastily assembling additional Confederate forces. Grant realized that he could not attack Vicksburg with Johnston threatening him from Jackson at his rear, so he decided to take Jackson first. Sherman's and McPherson's corps were assigned this task, which they accomplished with relative ease by May 14, driving Johnston's Jackson garrison out of town and farther eastward. Since Jackson was the Mississippi state capital, the morale factor in its capture was a major one.

The ease with which Jackson was taken was indicated by the fact that young Fred Grant, armed only with his father's dress sword and sash, rode unmolested into town astride his farm horse even before the Confederate flag was lowered over the state house. Knowing that it soon would be lowered and the Stars and Stripes raised in its place, Fred thought he might obtain the Confederate flag as a souvenir. He succeeded in reaching the state house, but was rudely brushed aside by a Union cavalry trooper who was hurrying to perform the flag ceremony. Disappointed but knowing there would be other souvenirs in the campaign that lay ahead, young Fred rode out to meet and greet the main body of Union troops who were just entering the town. Leading the conquering cavalcade was Fred's surprised but not wholly disapproving father. Years later, when Fred himself had graduated from West Point and was an army officer, he often laughingly reminded his father, who was then president of the United States, of how a twelve-year-old boy had led the Union armies into Jackson, Mississippi.

Grant's next move was to order McClernand's and McPherson's corps to turn about and move westward to attack Pemberton at Vicksburg. Sherman's corps was left in Jackson to destroy all Confederate supplies and communications and also to fend off any counterattack by Johnston.

Johnston had warned Pemberton not to let himself get bottled up inside Vicksburg, telling him that if he did, defeat was a foregone conclusion. Johnston, in fact, told Pemberton to forget about defending the city if he could escape with his army intact. But Pemberton had already been ordered by

Confederate commander in chief Lee to hold the key river city at any cost. This conflict in orders put Pemberton in an extremely difficult position, especially since his loyalty to the Confederate cause had already been questioned. Pemberton was a Northern general who, like Lee, had debated long and hard about which side to fight on in the war, but once he had made up his mind he was totally loyal to the South. His lack of generalship against Grant could be seriously questioned but never his loyalty.

Nevertheless, Pemberton decided to at least make a stand outside of Vicksburg before being driven inside the city. This he did at Champion's Hill and Black River Bridge on May 16 and 17. In both battles the Confederates were defeated, and they were finally forced to retreat inside the heavily fortified Gibraltar of the West, as Vicksburg was often called.

Hoping to capture Vicksburg by maintaining the sheer momentum of his advance, Grant sent savage attacks against it for the next several days, but once behind the barricades the Rebel defense stiffened and the Yankee attacks were beaten back with severe losses. After the last of these attacks, McClernand was highly critical of Grant and made the mistake of letting his criticism reach a Memphis newspaper. Grant asked McClernand if he had authorized the newspaper article, a copy of which Grant held in his hand. When McClernand admitted having done so, Grant relieved him from duty and shipped him back to Illinois. Major General Edward Ord replaced him.

Assault on Vicksburg. (U.S. ARMY)

General Sherman was no longer critical of Grant's Vicksburg campaign. With affairs in order at Jackson, Sherman briefly joined Grant when the siege of Vicksburg began. As the two men stood before the beleaguered city, Sherman said: "Until this moment I never thought your expedition a success. I never could see the end clearly until now. But this is a campaign. This is a success if we never take the town."

Sherman and Grant were always extremely close friends, and Sherman's loyalty was one of the reasons for that closeness. Grant was not unaware that earlier Sherman had said to a fellow officer: "I confess I don't like this roundabout project, but we must support Grant in whatever he undertakes." That, to Grant, was a true soldier speaking. And although he did not need Sherman's words to assure him the campaign had been a success—in less than three weeks and with no supply line his army had marched some 200 miles and won several victories—Grant deeply appreciated what for Sherman amounted to an abject apology.

Grant's reply, however, was gruff: "We'll take the town," he said.

Taking the town was merely a matter of time, for within days Grant's army had Vicksburg so tightly sealed off that, as one Union soldier wrote, "Not even a fly could get in or out." Both ammunition and food soon began to run low, and the civilian population suffered as much as the military both from hunger and the constant cannonading from

Grant's siege guns. Flour sold for as much as $1,000 a barrel and meat was $250 a pound. When cows, hogs, and dogs ran out, mule meat was all that was left for both civilians and soldiers to eat.

The one great Confederate hope was that Joe Johnston would eventually gather enough troops to smash through the Yankee lines and lift the siege. But Sherman successfully kept Johnston at bay.

As the siege continued, there was constant visiting back and forth between Yankee front-line troops and the Rebel defenders. Coffee and tobacco were exchanged as well as much good-natured banter. This fraternization between both sides was one of the strange things in the Civil War, contrasted as it was with the virtually mad slaughter that almost always followed once the fighting again began. On more than one occasion at Vicksburg it was discovered that soldiers in one army had relatives in the other, and arrangements were made for them to visit one another. On one occasion a Rebel soldier gave some money to his Yankee brother "to send to the folks back in Missouri."

But there was to be no renewed fighting in this campaign. Finally the word came through from Joe Johnston on June 15. "I consider saving Vicksburg hopeless," his wire read.

On July 1 Pemberton asked Grant for surrender terms. Knowing that it would be a major problem for the North to feed and care for Pemberton's huge captured army, Grant offered to parole all prisoners. Under the honor system then existing, paroled prisoners were not allowed to return to combat. Vicksburg was surrendered on July 4, Independence Day. Grant's losses were 9,400 in dead and wounded, while the Rebels lost 10,000 in dead and wounded plus 31,000 prisoners. Included among the latter were no less than 15 Confederate generals. Some 172 Confederate cannons were also captured, along with 60,000 rifles. These rifles were better than what most of Grant's men had, and they were promptly reissued to the Union troops. These were losses in men and material that the Confederacy could not afford.

On July 9 Union major general Nathaniel Banks, who had moved up from New Orleans with 15,000 men, captured Port Hudson, Louisiana, the last Confederate outpost on the Mississippi, just twenty-five miles north of Baton Rouge. Here another 6,000 Rebels were captured, but most important of all the Confederacy was now sliced in two, or as Lincoln said when he received the news that was joyous to the North: "The Father of Waters once more flows unvexed to the sea."

Grant's great victory at Vicksburg came simultaneously with a Federal victory in the East at Gettysburg. Together these twin triumphs sounded the death knell for the Confederacy.

But before this knell had sounded, Robert E. Lee had also scored a great victory, one that was as classic in both its conception and execution as Grant's had been at Vicksburg. This was the famous Battle of Chancellorsville.

PICKETT'S CHARGE

In the spring of 1863 the Army of the Potomac, this time under the handsome "Fighting Joe" Hooker, its fifth commander, once more moved against Richmond. Hooker had at his command more than 100,-000 seasoned troops, twice as many as Lee, who was stationed near Fredericksburg along the Rappahannock River guarding the railroad to the Confederate capital. Lee was seriously outnumbered because he had sent a major expedition under Longstreet into southeastern Virginia to gather supplies.

Hooker's plan of attack was relatively simple, and he was so sure of its success that he had boasted: "Only God can save the Confederates." Hooker sent Major General John Sedgwick and 40,000 men directly toward Fredericksburg, while Hooker himself led the rest of his army up the Rappahannock to Lee's left and rear to cut off the Confederate supply and communication lines. Hooker

119

General Joseph Hooker. (LIBRARY OF CONGRESS)

reasoned that Sedgwick's threatened frontal attack plus his own threat to the Confederate rear would force Lee to retreat. This retreat would run head-on into Hooker's enveloping forces, who would smash the Confederate Army of Northern Virginia once and for all. But Hooker, like so many Union generals before and afterward, reckoned without Robert E. Lee.

Hooker's campaign began smoothly, taking Lee completely by surprise. Lee had actually been thinking about another invasion of the North when on April 29, 1863, he found he was being threatened at both front and left rear. Any general but Lee might well have panicked, outnumbered as he was and facing complete envelopment. Instead, he calmly gave Major General Jubal "Jubalee" Early and 10,000 men the task of containing Sedgwick's thrust at Fredericksburg's Marye's Heights, and then turned the rest of his army around and sent it against Hooker.

Hooker was at a main road junction at Chancellorsville in the middle of a heavily wooded area called the Wilderness. If the Union commander had lived up to his Fighting Joe nickname, a Yankee victory would have been assured. Instead he suddenly lost his nerve, letting Sedgwick sit before Fredericksburg and placing the rest of his forces on the defensive at Chancellorsville. Lee and his able aide Stonewall Jackson instantly took advantage of Hooker's hesitancy.

Lee now divided his forces a third time! With

10,000 men under Early at Fredericksburg facing Sedgwick, Lee took command of 15,000 Rebels with which to face Hooker, and then sent the indomitable Jackson with 30,000 men on a lightning fifteen-mile march around Hooker's right flank to attack the Union army in the rear. In one bold stroke by Lee, Hooker had had his own plan reversed upon himself.

Jackson's swing around Hooker's right flank was partially screened by the tall timber in this wilderness area. These woods continued to hide Jackson's forces as they formed up to attack when their march was completed at five o'clock on the afternoon of May 2. Most of Hooker's men were in the midst of preparing their suppers over their campfires when the evening air was split by the fierce Rebel yell and the Rebels dashed out of the woods, firing as they came. Murderous hand-to-hand combat was the immediate result, and then the Yankee flank caved in and fell back in full retreat.

Jackson continued his attack until nightfall, when there was a considerable amount of confusion in both armies. Riding back through the Confederate lines after a reconnaissance mission, Jackson was accidentally fired upon by North Carolina's 33rd Infantry regiment and severely wounded in the arm. Major General A. P. Hill then took command, but he too was soon wounded and was replaced by cavalry leader Jeb Stuart.

The next day Stuart renewed the flank attack, and Lee also pressed forward on Hooker's front. In this action a Confederate artillery shell hit the house in Chancellorsville where Hooker had his headquarters and a piece of debris hit Hooker on the head. Dazed both by the blow and the bewildering Rebel attack, Hooker's further command of the battle was completely confused.

By this time Sedgwick had finally stormed Marye's Heights at Fredericksburg and started a drive to relieve Hooker in The Wilderness, but Lee calmly detached additional troops from his own command and sent them to his own rear to fend off Sedgwick. Having now managed to join his own forces with Jackson's former troops now led by Stuart, Lee was making preparations to mount a full-scale attack against Hooker. But Hooker had regained his senses enough to realize that he wanted no more of Lee. Thoroughly beaten, Hooker withdrew his Army of the Potomac back toward Washington.

By outthinking, outmaneuvering, outflanking, and outfighting Hooker in a battle in which he had been taken by surprise and in which he was seriously outnumbered, Lee had fought his most brilliant battle. And if one Rebel could beat two Yankees, reasoned Lee and Jefferson Davis, certainly a final Confederate victory in the East was a foregone conclusion.

But Lee had suffered one loss in the Battle of Chancellorsville that was irreparable and would eventually lead to his defeat at Gettysburg. Shortly after Stonewall Jackson had been wounded, it had been necessary for surgeons to amputate his arm,

Confederate dead at Marye's Heights. (LIBRARY OF CONGRESS)

and on May 10 he died. Lee's words when he had heard about Jackson's amputation now proved prophetic. "Tell him to get well and come back to me as soon as he can," Lee said. "He has lost his left arm, but I have lost my right."

During this period General Lee himself was not a well man. In March he had suffered a mild heart attack but had recovered sufficiently to command brilliantly at Chancellorsville. After that battle he was stricken with an attack of dysentery, a common but nonetheless serious complaint among the men in both armies. Nevertheless, by mid-May he had recovered sufficiently to travel to Richmond and consult with President Davis about future Confederate military plans.

At this time Davis was under great pressure to release one of Lee's divisions led by Major General George Pickett and use it to reinforce the Confederates fighting in the West. Lee, however, persuaded Davis that a successful invasion of Pennsylvania's rich farm country could lead to the fall of Baltimore, Washington, and Philadelphia and cause the collapse of the Federal government. But to make such an attack Lee would need every last man in the Army of Northern Virginia. So Pickett remained with Lee and went on to undying military fame.

On June 3 the Confederates moved down the Shenandoah and Cumberland valleys toward Maryland and then Pennsylvania. As the Rebel infantry moved out, the colorful Jeb Stuart held a spectacular cavalry review at Brandy Station, Virginia. This review was the first event in what was to prove an unfortunate chain of circumstances for the Confederacy. Shortly after it was over, Stuart's cavalry was struck by a corps of Union cavalry commanded by Major General Alfred Pleasonton, who had been sent out by General Hooker to find out if Lee's army was indeed marching north. The clash between Stuart's and Pleasonton's cavalry corps, each numbering about 10,000 troopers, was the biggest pure cavalry action of the war and the last such saber-swinging engagement by men on horseback anywhere in the world. In it the Union cavalry came of age. Up to then it had been regarded as far inferior to the Confederate cavalry, but at Brandy Station Union troopers earned the full respect of the Rebels. While the Union horsemen did not defeat the Confederate cavalry, they almost did and Stuart's reputation was badly tarnished. Both sides suffered severe casualties, the Union almost 1,000 and the Confederacy more than 500. Among the latter was Rooney Lee, General Lee's son, whose leg was badly gashed by a saber stroke.

Pleasonton's cavalry scouting expedition had been completely successful in being able to report to Hooker that Lee's entire army was headed for Pennsylvania. Hooker then ordered his army to cross the Potomac and also head north. Partly to refurbish his reputation, Jeb Stuart decided to take off on yet one more wild ride around the entire Northern army and report its movements back to Lee. This venture kept Stuart out of the forthcoming Gettysburg battle until its second day, but worst of all, Stuart allowed the Army of the Potomac to get between him and Lee, and for ten days Stuart was unable to give Lee any information at all. With the "eyes" of his army thus blinded, Lee had to advance virtually in the dark. On June 28, however, Lee received word from another source that the Army of the Potomac was on the move to confront him in Pennsylvania. He also learned that the Potomac forces had yet one more new commander.

General Hooker had been reluctant to begin a new campaign without major reinforcements. When these were not forthcoming, Hooker submitted his resignation. Since Lincoln had wanted to get rid of Hooker but for political reasons did not want to be the one to officially relieve him, he quickly accepted Hooker's resignation. In his place he named Major General George G. Meade.

Meade had fought well in all the major battles in the East since the start of the war and had been wounded in the Peninsular Campaign. His one major fault was a fiery temper that kept him in hot water with both his subordinates and his superiors. On the very day he was named to command the Army of the Potomac Meade had had a bitter argument with Hooker. That night, when a messenger from the Union War Department arrived to tell Meade he had been promoted, Meade at first thought he had been placed under arrest! Even so, he was not exactly overjoyed when he realized he had been placed in charge of an army that was al-

General George Meade. (LIBRARY OF CONGRESS)

ready committed to a campaign he had not planned. Nevertheless, he quietly accepted the responsibility, making very few changes in Hooker's strategy. Meade would have preferred to fight a defensive battle at Frederick, Maryland, but his army was already on the move and destined to clash with Lee in Pennsylvania. One of the curious things about the Battle of Gettysburg was that neither Meade nor Lee expected or particularly wanted to fight a major engagement there.

By the time Lee's advancing army reached Pennsylvania it was strung out between York and Chambersburg, a distance of some fifty miles. Late on the afternoon of June 30, Union cavalry clashed with advance elements of Lee's army a few miles west of Gettysburg. Having had no word from Jeb Stuart, Lee did not know right up until this moment exactly where Meade was. When he realized that the Union cavalry were scouting out ahead of Meade's entire main army, the Confederate commander immediately realized he must concentrate his own widely scattered army. The logical place to do this was at Gettysburg, with its major junction of a dozen roads. Meade himself was not yet at Gettysburg, but he knew immediately that he must prevent Lee from bringing his scattered forces together there. The first minor clashes between small elements of both armies soon grew into a major battle. When it began, neither commander knew the strength of the other's army. Actually Meade commanded about 120,000 men, and Lee about 90,000.

The next day, July 1, a corps of dismounted Union cavalrymen fought a delaying action northwest of Gettysburg against Confederates led by Major General A. P. Hill and Lieutenant General Richard Ewell. Despite the fact that they were armed with new eight-shot Spencer repeating rifles, the Yankee troopers were badly outfought by Hill's and Ewell's forces and were driven back through the streets of Gettysburg. By late afternoon they had taken up defensive positions at a point called Cemetery Hill.

Lee immediately ordered an attack against Cemetery Hill, but Ewell and Hill both delayed until it was too dark to fight. During the night Meade not only reinforced Cemetery Hill with several infantry divisions but also occupied nearby Culp's Hill on his right and heavily fortified Cemetery Ridge on his left. Lee's opportunity for quickly winning a decisive victory at Gettysburg had escaped him.

At dawn on July 2 Lee ordered a full-scale attack at both ends of the extended Union line, but again the Confederate advance was delayed and did not begin until midafternoon. This time Rebel general Longstreet was mainly to blame for the delay. Longstreet had arrived late at the battle scene on the previous day, and when he did arrive he wanted to circle around Meade rather than attack him directly. Lee pointed at the Union positions and said, "The enemy is there, and I mean to fight him there." When ordered to attack at dawn the next day, Longstreet said, "I never go into battle with one boot off." His so-called other boot was General Pickett's division. Pickett and his men finally arrived at three o'clock, and Longstreet's command swept forward.

But Meade had been using every spare moment to add strength to his defensive forces as well as to their fortified positions, and the Confederates encountered a storm of fire from rifles and artillery. As Longstreet struck the south end of the Union line and Ewell attacked to the north, there were deadly fights in a wheat field, a peach orchard, a rocky area called the Devil's Den, and up the slopes of a hill called Little Round Top. Little Round Top was a key artillery position, and the fighting there was so fierce that when both attacking Rebel and defending Yankee infantrymen ran out of ammunition they threw rocks at one another. The position was finally denied to the Confederates, a turning point in the battle, since Rebel artillery on this hill could have smashed the Yankee breastworks. At Cemetery Hill and Culp's Hill the Confederate attack pressed forward until well after darkness. But when the day's fighting finally died down, the Federal forces still held their badly battered positions. Nothing had been decided except the fate of thousands of men who had died during the battles.

The next day, July 3, Lee decided to make an all-out attack against the very center of the Union line. Interestingly, Meade knew that this was exactly what Lee would do, because it was the only thing he had left to do—except perhaps to withdraw, and Lee would never withdraw as long as there was one chance left. Lee had unsuccessfully attacked both of

Breastworks at Little Round Top, Gettysburg. (LIBRARY OF CONGRESS, BRADY COLLECTION)

Dead Confederate soldier at Little Round Top, Gettysburg. (LIBRARY OF CONGRESS, PHOTO BY ALEXANDER GARDNER)

Meade's flanks; now he would try the center. And Meade knew this attack would also fail, and wondered if Lee knew it too. As Meade told his staff officers, there seemed something almost fated about this final, desperate assault.

On the crucial day of the Battle of Gettysburg, Lee was suffering severely from dysentery. Nevertheless, he conferred with his generals about just how the final, all-out attack against the Union center should be made.

Longstreet was firmly against making the attack. When he looked at the strong Union fortifications along Cemetery Ridge and saw the long valley through which the Rebels would have to advance before reaching those fortifications, Longstreet said to Lee: "General, I have been a soldier all of my life. I have been with soldiers engaged in combat by couples, by squads, companies, regiments, and armies, and I should know as well as any man what soldiers can do. It is my opinion that no 15,000 men ever arrayed for battle can take that position."

But Lee ordered the attack to go forward.

Lee's plan was simple enough. Following a heavy Confederate artillery bombardment which would silence the Federal defensive cannons and soften the Federal entrenched positions, four divisions from Longstreet's and Hill's commands would make a massive frontal assault directly against the Union center. The 15,000-man assault force was under the command of General Pickett.

Major General Winfield S. Hancock was in direct

charge of the Union defenders, who numbered about 10,000. Although the Federal troops were outnumbered at the point of attack, ample reserves were nearby. In addition, Hancock's men were firing from behind wooden and stone breastworks and walls, and there would be nothing but raw courage to protect the advancing Confederates. This advance would have to be made right out in the open where both artillery and rifle fire could be perfectly zeroed in on the lines of doomed Rebels. Although they, too, knew it was going to happen, many Yankee defenders could not really believe the Confederates would try such an attack.

The day was blistering hot. It began with the scattered sounds of rifle shots from both sides that occasionally grew into heavy fire. Here and there on the battlefield there were small, quick skirmishes that had no particular meaning except that in each of them men died or were wounded. Suddenly, at midday, a heavy silence fell over the battlefield.

The silence seemed interminable to the waiting soldiers, both those who were about to die and those who were about to kill them. Then Longstreet ordered the Confederate artillery to go into action, and 160 guns roared the opening barrage. The 100 Union defensive artillery guns instantly replied. It was the heaviest barrage of the war thus far, and it seemed that nothing could live under it. But when it ended two hours later, the Federal infantry was still in place, and the Federal artillery was still ready for continued action.

Silence once again fell over the battlefield, and then the long lines of Confederate infantrymen began to roll forward. Pickett had gone directly to Longstreet to ask him for an order to begin the infantry attack, but Longstreet was so convinced that Pickett was leading his men to needless slaughter that he couldn't speak. Instead, he simply bowed his head.

"Sir," Pickett said, "I shall lead my division forward."

To the waiting Federal forces on Cemetery Ridge the truly incredible thing about Pickett's advancing lines was that they came on in perfect formation, each man dressing on, or lining up evenly with, the man at his right as if they were on parade.

The parade formation lasted only until the Rebels came within range. Then open spaces began to appear in the ranks of gray as Yankee riflemen found their marks. Federal cannons also found their range, and soon great gaps began to appear in the lines of steadily advancing men. But when these gaps appeared, they were quickly closed by the drill-perfect Confederates, who continued to dress right as if on a peacetime march.

When Pickett's Charge began, the Rebel line was about a mile wide. As it continued and the men closed in to fill the gaps, this front narrowed, but it continued to roll forward unhesitatingly. Then, here and there, the charge began to falter. Officers on horseback, Pickett in the lead, brandished their swords and waved their men forward. And despite the fact that they marched directly in the face of withering rifle fire and canister shot from cannons fired at close range, some of Pickett's men, the Rebel yell on their lips, managed to charge right up and over the Federal breastworks. Here there was mad hand-to-hand combat, especially at one point called the Angle, but in the end every Rebel who made it over the Yankee breastworks was either cut down with the Rebel yell on his dying lips or captured. What some were to call "the high tide of the Confederacy" had reached its peak on Cemetery Ridge, and it now began to roll back.

As the Rebel tide receded back down the valley, Lee rode forward on Traveller and tried to rally his men against a possible Union counterattack. When he encountered General Pickett, who had miraculously escaped unhurt from the thick of the fight, Lee insisted that Pickett halt the remnants of his retreating division and prepare defensive positions.

"General Lee," Pickett said sorrowfully, "I have no division now."

About half of the gallant host that made its way up the valley made its way back down again.

There was no Federal counterattack, for the Union forces had suffered grievously also. In the entire three-day holocaust the Union army suffered 23,000 casualties and the Confederates 28,000. This was virtually a third of Lee's entire army, a loss which he could not absorb and continue waging offensive war in Northern territory. He had no choice but to retreat into Virginia. Meade made no

Union dead at Gettysburg. (LIBRARY OF CONGRESS, PHOTO BY T. H. O'SULLIVAN)

immediate effort to follow the defeated Confederates, a fact that President Lincoln could not understand.

"We had them in our grasp." the president said. "We had only to stretch out our hands, and they were ours. But nothing I could say or do could make the army move."

But Lincoln's disappointment and irritation were to be smoothed away by Grant's victory at Vicksburg, as well as by other Union successes, and some weeks later, on November 19, 1863, he delivered his immortal Gettysburg Address on the site of what would be remembered as perhaps the most famous battle of the Civil War.

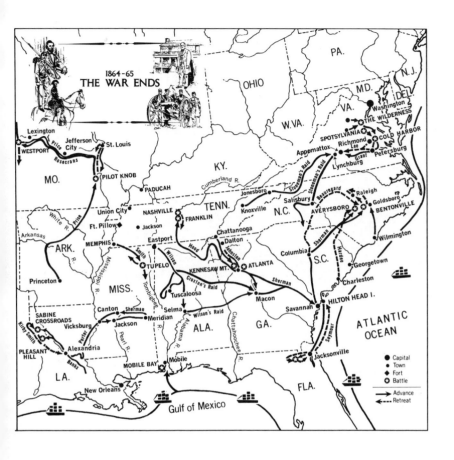

1864-65
THE WAR ENDS

Capital ●
Town •
Fort ◆
Battle ✪
Advance →
Retreat ◄----

LINCOLN FINDS
HIS GENERAL

Up to this point in the nation's history the rank of lieutenant general had been held by only two United States Army officers—George Washington and Winfield Scott. Then, on March 9, 1864, a third officer was given this rank. He was Ulysses S. Grant, who was also named general in chief of the Union armies. Frustrated by a whole series of Union commanders—Scott, McClellan, Pope, Burnside, Hooker, and Meade—Lincoln finally turned to the man who would win the major decisive victories and end the war. Lincoln had found his general.

Between the time of Grant's victory at Vicksburg and his appointment as general in chief, the Union had suffered a major defeat—the Battle of Chickamauga—and a major victory—the Battle of Chattanooga—in the West. Major action had shifted there after Gettysburg, which left Lee's and Meade's armies too exhausted to engage in anything except indecisive skirmishes with each other.

After the Vicksburg campaign Union major general William Rosecrans in Tennessee had forced Confederate major general Braxton Bragg out of Chattanooga and into northern Georgia. But Rosecrans, who was affectionately called "Old Rosy" by his men, was far too rosy in his outlook regarding Bragg's retreating Rebels. Old Rosy thought they were in a complete panic. Suddenly, however, Bragg's forces, supported by Longstreet's division which Lee had sent west, turned and in mid-September 1863 struck Rosecrans' army at Chickamauga Creek, Georgia, just fifteen miles south of Chattanooga, and almost destroyed it. The only thing that prevented its complete destruction was a heroic defensive stand by a Union corps led by Major General George Thomas, an effort that gave Thomas his nickname, "The Rock of Chickamauga."

After Chickamauga, Rosecrans' Army of the Cumberland retreated into Chattanooga, where it was hemmed in by both the surrounding Appalachian Mountains and the Confederates. The situation there soon developed into a grim siege, with the Yankees unable to get out and the Rebels unable to get in. The Yankees could probably be starved out, however, and this the Rebels resolutely set out to accomplish. At this point Grant took charge of the situation.

"After Chickamauga," President Lincoln said, "Rosecrans acted like a duck hit on the head." But, as was Lincoln's way, he did not want to personally remove the popular Old Rosy. Instead he placed

Grant in command of all the western armies and let him do the job.

Grant did not take long to act. He replaced Rosecrans with Rock-of-Chickamauga Thomas and named Sherman to take over the Federal Army of the Tennessee, which he himself had formerly commanded. Grant was also reinforced by 20,000 men from General Meade's Army of the Potomac. These men, under General Hooker, were sent to Tennessee by rail, a 1,200-mile journey that was accomplished in the then-record time of eight days.

Bragg's troops surrounding Chattanooga held key positions on Lookout Mountain and along Missionary Ridge. Before these positions could be assaulted Grant knew he must begin getting supplies to the besieged men inside the city. This he did by using General Hooker's newly arrived men to open up what the hungry troops called "the cracker line" through several mountain passes. By November Grant was ready to resume the offensive. He had about 60,000 men; the Confederates, 40,000.

Hooker stormed and took Lookout Mountain on November 24 in a battle that was not so difficult as it was spectacular. Bragg apparently thought the mountain could be easily defended and had only a handful of men stationed there. Hooker's attacking troops easily overran the defenders and planted the Union flag atop Lookout Mountain. During the first part of the Union advance the mountain was obscured by low-lying clouds. But as it continued some of these clouds rolled away, and soon the action was clearly visible to war correspondents looking on from below. They promptly began calling it the Battle Above the Clouds.

The most important action was at Missionary Ridge, where the Confederates were dug in in a series of trenches. These trenches were stormed by many of the men who had retreated in panic at Chickamauga, and whom Thomas' stout defenders had been taunting unmercifully for running away ever since.

General Thomas was in charge of the Missionary Ridge assault, and Grant had told him to take only the trenches at the base of the ridge and then regroup for a final move forward. The angry Union men dutifully took the first series of trenches but then in a frenzied rush proceeded to charge on up the steep face of the ridge, driving the Rebels before them.

Coming on this action, Grant demanded of Thomas: "By whose authority are those men up there, sir?"

Looking through his field glasses, Thomas replied slowly: "I gather by their own authority, General."

Grant watched silently for a moment. Then he ordered reinforcements onto Missionary Ridge, and soon the Rebels were in the first full-scale, panic-stricken retreat the Yankees had ever seen. "My God, look at 'em run!" was the awed comment of more than one onlooker.

The Battle of Chattanooga placed the entire

Lookout Mountain, site of the Battle Above the Clouds. (LIBRARY OF CONGRESS)

West in Union hands. Actually it meant the Confederacy had lost the war, but surrender never crossed Jefferson Davis' mind. When Grant was called to Washington, however, to be promoted to lieutenant general and named general in chief of the Union armies, both Davis and Lee knew they were facing a bulldog opponent who would fight without letup to destroy the Confederate armies. From now to its conclusion this would be total war.

Grant wanted no part of Washington and its politics. He decided to make his headquarters with Meade's army in the field near Culpeper Court House in Virginia. Thus, although Meade remained in command of the Army of the Potomac, it gradually came to be regarded as Grant's army.

Davis and Lee had been correct. Grant planned to hit the Confederates on all fronts at once and without letup. The Army of the Potomac would attack Lee's army in northern Virginia. Major General Benjamin Butler and his Army of the James River would attempt to capture Richmond by advancing from Fort Monroe up the Virginia peninsula as McClellan had tried to do. In the Shenandoah Valley a diversionary force under Major General Franz Sigel would attempt to draw Confederate defenders away from Richmond. In the West, Sherman with three armies now at his command was to invade Georgia and destroy the South's will to fight by disrupting the source of its main food supply.

Grant set all these military wheels in motion in May 1864.

In the East there quickly followed a second battle in the Wilderness near Chancellorsville, one at Spotsylvania, and one at Cold Harbor. In the first of these three battles Grant was beaten as badly as Hooker had been a year earlier in the same area, but he refused to retreat. Instead, he kept the pressure relentlessly on Lee by temporarily withdrawing and then advancing once more against Lee's left flank, a maneuver which led to the Spotsylvania conflict.

In the Spotsylvania campaign Major General Phil Sheridan, who had been brought east by Grant to lead the Army of the Potomac's cavalry corps, met and defeated Jeb Stuart's Rebel cavalry at Yellow Tavern near Richmond. In this engagement the colorful Stuart was killed.

Infantry fighting at and around the Spotsylvania Court House crossroads lasted twelve days, from May 8 to 19, and was some of the bloodiest fighting in this or any other war. At one point called the Bloody Angle, Yankees and Rebel troops engaged in hand-to-hand combat for the entire last day of the battle. At another crucial stage of the conflict Lee himself was about to lead a charge astride Traveller but was persuaded not to by his troops. The outcome of the struggle was in the end indecisive, but Grant once again partially disengaged and then renewed the attack by attempting to outflank Lee to the left. This brought about the Battle of Cold Harbor, an area within the Richmond city defenses. Here, on June 3, Grant ordered an assault at the center of Lee's eight-mile-long defensive line and

General Philip H. Sheridan (U.S. SIGNAL CORPS PHOTO, NATIONAL ARCHIVES, BRADY COLLECTION)

General Grant and his staff hold a conference. (LIBRARY OF
CONGRESS)

was bloodily repulsed. After the war Grant said it was an attack he never should have ordered.

Up to this point in what amounted to a continuing running battle the casualties were enormous— 60,000 for the Union and almost as many for the Confederacy. The South could not continue to suffer such casualties and survive because it was simply running out of replacements. Even the North, with its huge manpower pool, was hard-put to provide Grant with replacements. Having expected Grant to be something of a miracle worker when he took command of the Union armies, Northern newspapers and the public now began to refer to him as the Butcher and clamor for his dismissal.

But, whether they had realized it before or not, this was the way Grant fought. And whether it was the right way or the wrong way, in the end it would prevail. "I plan," Grant wrote in a grim report to Lincoln, "to fight it out on this line if it takes all summer."

Meanwhile, things had not gone especially well with Sigel's forces in the Shenandoah Valley or with Butler's forces moving up the Virginia peninsula from the south. Sigel was unable to draw any defenders away from Richmond, and Butler was unable to reach the Rebel capital. Sigel was kept at bay by a relatively small number of Rebel volunteers, among whom were the teen-aged student cadets of the Virginia Military Institute. These brave young cadets helped defeat Sigel at New Market. Ben Butler let himself get sealed up by General Beauregard "like a cork in a bottle," as Grant put it, on a small peninsula called the Bermuda Head, and was of little immediate use.

Grant now found himself in a position somewhat similar to that of McClellan two years earlier. Beyond the Chickahominy River he and his men could see the spires of Richmond, but the city itself seemed unattainable.

At this point Grant made another bold maneuver, again to his left. Evacuating his positions at Cold Harbor in mid-June, he crossed the James River east of Richmond and attacked Petersburg. Petersburg was the key railroad center leading to Richmond from the south, and its capture would strangle the Confederate capital. But before Grant could get there Lee had reinforced the city, and Grant then settled down at City Point, from which Petersburg could be besieged. This situation was somewhat similar to that at Vicksburg, but the result was by no means a foregone conclusion.

SHERMAN'S MARCH
TO THE SEA

When Grant and Meade and the Army of the Potomac began their campaign against Lee's Army of Northern Virginia in the spring of 1864, Sherman began his campaign against Joe Johnston and his Confederate Army of the Tennessee. Sherman's immediate goal was Atlanta, Georgia. He had at his command 105,000 men. Johnston, who was supported by Lieutenant General Leonidas Polk, had 65,000 men. When Sherman started his advance, Johnston—well aware that he was seriously outnumbered—decided to fight a major delaying action.

The main reason for Johnston's delaying tactics had to do with politics. President Lincoln was facing an election in the fall of 1864, and the Northern public had grown weary of the war. If Lee could hold out in the East and Johnston could hold out in the West, Lincoln might well lose the election. If he did, the new president would certainly sue for

151

General William Tecumseh Sherman. (U.S. SIGNAL CORPS PHOTO, NATIONAL ARCHIVES, BRADY COLLECTION)

peace, because he would be none other than General George B. McClellan, who was Lincoln's political opponent. The Democrats, controlled by the Copperheads in their party, had nominated McClellan, whose war aims left little doubt that he would agree to end the conflict if elected.

But the South was also weary of the war, and the pendulum of Southern sympathy had begun to swing away from Jefferson Davis. With Davis out of office, perhaps a new Confederate president could make peace with the North. For this reason, and because Davis failed to see the military wisdom in Johnston's delaying actions, Johnston was suddenly relieved of his command and replaced by Major General John B. Hood. This move delighted Sherman, who knew that Hood was the kind of general who would either attack or stand still and fight.

Actually Johnston's tactics had been quite successful against Sherman. Between early May, when Sherman had started his campaign, and July, when Johnston was relieved, the Union Army had advanced only 100 miles and had suffered at least one sharp setback at Kenesaw Mountain. In addition, Johnston still had a stout hold on Atlanta. Now, however, Hood came out from behind the strong Atlanta fortifications and attacked Sherman at Peach Tree Creek. Sherman beat off this attack as well as a second one and forced Hood back inside the city. Hood remained bottled up there until September 1, while Sherman cut the railroads leading into the city and began to prepare fortifications for a siege. On September 2 Hood saw that the game was up and evacuated the city, retreating into northwest Alabama. Sherman wired Grant: "Atlanta is ours and fairly won!"

Grant ordered that a 100-gun salute be fired when he received the news, but it was President Lincoln who was truly overjoyed. Lincoln himself had not expected to be reelected on November 8, but the fall of Atlanta, he knew, would also bring about the fall of McClellan in the battle of the ballots. Lincoln judged correctly. He was reelected by 212 electoral votes to McClellan's 21. The war would be prosecuted to its final military, not political, conclusion.

Meanwhile, Sherman started out on his final major campaign in the South—a campaign that would earn him undying military fame throughout the North and undying hatred throughout the South. This was his devastating march from Atlanta to the Atlantic seaboard.

The march to the sea was Sherman's idea, and it was not an idea of which either Lincoln or Grant wholly approved. They both thought that Sherman's main mission should be the destruction of Hood's army. But Sherman was persuasive in his arguments. He reasoned that the quickest way to end the war was to destroy the Confederacy's economy—its farms, factories, supply depots, and railroads—in a wide swath between Atlanta and Savannah. Sherman knew that the food he destroyed was badly needed by Lee's men in Petersburg and Richmond. He would let Hood's army go where it pleased. He assumed that this would be north. If so, General Thomas at Nashville could handle Hood. To make sure he could, Sherman would reinforce Thomas with 30,000 men from his own forces. But with the rest of his command—more than 60,000 men—Sherman would strike a death blow at the heartland of the Confederacy.

To make his march, Sherman would have to cut off his communications and supply lines and live off the land—a lesson he had learned from Grant in the Vicksburg campaign. And, Sherman reminded Grant, laying waste to the Southern economy had already been partially accomplished in the summer and fall of 1864 by Phil Sheridan in the Shenandoah Valley. When the siege of Petersburg had extended into weeks and months, Grant himself had ordered Sheridan into the Shenandoah Valley with specific orders not only to defeat the Rebel forces there but also to destroy all of that fertile valley's crops. These crops furnished Richmond with vital food for both civilians and soldiers and forage for the soldiers' horses. Sheridan had accomplished his mission well, defeating Jubal Early at Winchester, Fisher's Hill, and Cedar Creek, and turning the Shenandoah farmland into a wasteland. Mounted on his huge horse named Rienzi, little Phil Sheridan had become the scourge of the Shenandoah Valley. Sherman proposed to become the scourge of Georgia.

Lincoln and Grant finally approved Sherman's plan "to make Georgia howl," and the march to the sea began in mid-November.

Sherman's troops destroying railway lines at Atlanta. (LIBRARY OF CONGRESS)

Destroyed railway station at Atlanta. (LIBRARY OF CONGRESS)

Sherman's men left Atlanta in flames. They had been ordered to destroy all the factories and military installations in the city, and in the course of carrying out these orders many private homes and places of business were set on fire. Little but ashes was left.

Sherman's march soon took on all of the atmosphere of vandals on a destructive picnic. Since they were not threatened by any enemy soldiers, Sherman's soldiers soon shed all vestiges of military discipline. They happily carried out Sherman's orders to destroy all crops, barns, cotton gins, cattle, railroads, and warehouses along the route of their march. They also gorged themselves on hams, poultry, and any other food they could appropriate for themselves. In addition, they seemed to assume that their mission gave them a license to steal, and looting was widespread. The sixty-mile-wide swath of total destruction cut through the Georgia countryside by Sherman's marauding men was something a civilian population would not see again until the total wars of the twentieth century.

Sherman's march to the sea ended on December 21, 1864, with the capture of Savannah. In a wire to President Lincoln, Sherman offered the coastal city to the nation as a Christmas present.

Meanwhile, General Thomas had indeed been able to handle Hood when Hood invaded Tennessee, and by the end of the year had driven him back out of the state in complete disorder.

But the siege of Petersburg went on. It lasted in

fact for nine long months, from June 19, 1864, to April 2, 1865. During its course Lee's army constructed an elaborate series of defensive trenches, and Grant's and Meade's army constructed an equally elaborate series of trenches from which to conduct their offensive operations. In many ways the battle conditions that resulted were a forerunner of the stalemated trench warfare that was to occur on the Western Front in World War I.*

At one point in the siege of Petersburg a novel method was used by the Union to attempt to breach the Rebel defenses and thus break the stalemate. At the suggestion of Lieutenant Colonel Henry Pleasonton of the 48th Pennsylvania Regiment, which was mainly made up of coal miners, a huge tunnel was dug from the Union lines to a point directly beneath the Confederate trenches. The far end of this tunnel was packed with several tons of explosives. When these explosives were ignited they were expected to blow up a large area of the Confederate defensive trenches, and Union troops would thus be enabled to pour through this opening and overrun the stunned defenders.

The great Petersburg mine was successfully exploded in late July 1864, but it created such a huge crater with such steep slopes that it soon became a slaughter pit. Union attackers who entered it could not get out and were helpless targets for Confederate gunners. In the end it cost the Union some 4,000

*See another book in this series, *The United States in World War I.*

A Union artillery battery under fire at Petersburg. (U.S. SIGNAL CORPS PHOTO, NATIONAL ARCHIVES, BRADY COLLECTION)

Ruins of Richmond. During the evacuation of Richmond, residents burned a large part of the city's business section rather than let it fall intact to the Union army. (LIBRARY OF CONGRESS)

casualties and accomplished nothing except to set a record as the loudest single explosion of the war.

Actually, the Petersburg defenses never did fall. Lee simply abandoned them, as well as Richmond, in the spring of 1865. He was forced to do so when his sources of supplies were completely cut off. Sheridan in the Shenandoah Valley and Sherman in Georgia had cut off Lee's domestic sources of supplies. A trickle of aid had continued to reach Lee from Europe via Wilmington, North Carolina, which was a port for blockade runners. But early in 1865 the port of Wilmington was closed by an amphibious expedition led by Major General Alfred Terry and Rear Admiral David Porter. This sealed both the port and the fate of Lee's Army of Northern Virginia.

When Lee abandoned Petersburg and Richmond on April 2, 1865, he tried to make his way to North Carolina and join forces with Joe Johnston, who had been given a new command there after being relieved at Atlanta. But Grant continued his bulldog tactics, hanging on Lee's left flank and causing the Confederate army to wander almost helplessly westward. In addition, Sherman had now begun to march northward from Savannah to join Grant's and Meade's Army of the Potomac, so that Lee was about to be caught in a huge military vise. Johnston did his brave best to fend off the relentlessly advancing Sherman, and Lee—his army now out of rations—did his brave and final best to escape the bulldog Grant harrying his flanks. But Grant now at long last had Lee in the open and he would not be denied.

Grant sent Phil Sheridan's cavalry galloping out in front of Lee to head him off. This Sheridan accomplished, cutting across immediately in front of Lee's defeated yet still advancing army at a Virginia village just eighty miles west of Petersburg. The name of the village was Appomattox Court House.

"NOTHING LEFT BUT TO SEE GENERAL GRANT"

A man by the name of Wilmer McLean had a modest home at Bull Run Creek near the site of the first major battle of the Civil War. By a curious coincidence the McLean home, this time at Appomattox Court House, was the site of one of the last scenes in the Civil War. For safety's sake McLean had moved his family to Appomattox after the Bull Run conflict, little realizing that two of the great opposing armies would converge there as the war drew to a close. When Lee's lieutenants were seeking a place where Lee and Grant could meet to discuss the surrender of the Army of Northern Virginia, McLean volunteered the use of his house.

Lee and Grant met at the McLean home on Palm Sunday, April 9, 1865. They had gotten together after an exchange of messages during the last several days of fighting in the Appomattox Court House area. Lee had been desperately fending off every Union thrust, hoping against hope for some last-minute military miracle. But when even his most trusted lieutenants told him that further fighting would be futile, Lee said: "Then there is nothing left for me to do but go and see General Grant, and I would rather die a thousand deaths."

General Lee, dressed immaculately in his best uniform with a silk sash around his waist and wearing a beautiful dress-parade sword, arrived at the McLean house half an hour before Grant. Grant, whose baggage had gone astray during the fighting, arrived wearing his usual rumpled uniform with a private's blouse for a coat. He wore no sword, his only insignia of rank being the shoulder straps and stars on his blouse.

The two men presented an enormous contrast: the tall, regal Lee in his formal uniform and the stumpy, informal Grant in his mud-spattered fighting attire. Lee, at fifty-eight, was also the older of the two men, his sixteen-year seniority showing in the gray of his neatly trimmed hair and beard. Grant's unkempt beard was a ruddy chestnut color. But the contrast was only an outward one. Both men were great generals. They had proved that fact during four years of war. In addition, both men were great human beings. They proved that on this Palm Sunday morning.

One of Lee's lieutenants had suggested to Lee that rather than surrender, they should scatter and take to the woods, where they would be "as hard to catch as rabbits and partridges." Guerrilla warfare throughout the South would keep the Federal government futilely occupied for years. But Lee would have none of this. "We must consider the effect on the country as a whole," he said. "Already it is demoralized by the four years of war. If I took your advice, the men would become mere bands of marauders, and the enemy's cavalry would pursue them and overrun many wide sections of the country they may otherwise have no occasion to visit. We would bring on a state of affairs it would take the country many years to recover from."

And Grant's surrender terms were equally statesmanlike. He was no longer "Unconditional Surrender" Grant but a man who looked to the peacetime years ahead. All of Lee's army was to be paroled. They would be allowed simply to stack their arms and return to their homes without further penalty. Perhaps noting General Lee's dress sword, Grant not only made a point of not asking Lee for it but also wrote into the surrender terms a stipulation that permitted all officers to keep their side arms, horses, and baggage. Although he did not include it in the formal surrender document, Grant also said he knew that most of Lee's enlisted men were farmers, and he would tell his officers to allow Rebel troops to claim their own horses and take them home with them for use in plowing.

"This will have the best possible effect upon the men," Lee said quietly. "It will do much toward conciliating our people."

Grant also told Lee he would immediately make 25,000 rations available for Lee's hungry troops. Again Lee thanked him, the two men shook hands, and Lee departed—staring straight ahead, his face

Surrender site at Appomattox Court House, Virginia. (LIBRARY OF CONGRESS, PHOTO BY T. H. O'SULLIVAN)

haggard with grief. Outside, he pulled on his gauntlets, pounded a fist into one palm, mounted Traveller, and rode off slowly and silently through the throngs of cheering men who were the remnants of the gallant gray Army of Northern Virginia.

Confederate General Joe Johnston surrendered his forces to General Sherman on April 26 at Raleigh, North Carolina, on terms identical with those of Lee's surrender to Grant. Scattered fighting went on until May 26, but with Lee's and Johnston's surrenders the war was indeed over.

But even after Appomattox the madness continued.

President Lincoln was shot by a mad actor, John Wilkes Booth, at Ford's Theater on Good Friday, April 14, 1865. He died the next day. The assassin had also planned to kill General Grant, who had been invited with his wife to attend the theater with the Lincolns but went instead to visit the Grant children, who were in school at Burlington, New Jersey.

Confederate president Jefferson Davis had refused to give himself up even after the Confederacy collapsed. Attempting to flee the country, he was captured on May 10 at Irwinsville, Georgia, and imprisoned at Fort Monroe, Virginia. Davis was accused of plotting the assassination of Lincoln and was confined to Fort Monroe for two years, despite the fact that not a single shred of evidence was ever discovered connecting him with the assassination. On May 13, 1867, he was released on $100,000 bail, and in 1869 the charges against him were dropped.

About 1 million men were killed or wounded

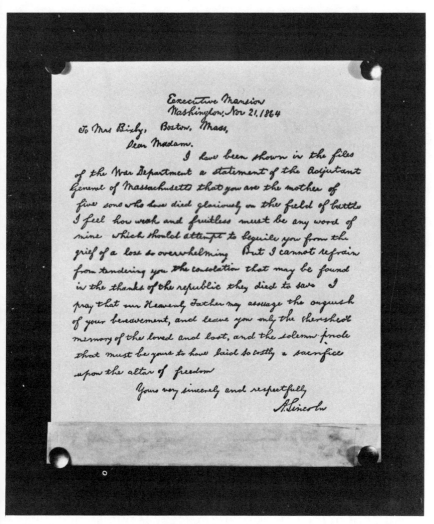

Lincoln's letter to a mother who lost five sons in the war.
(NATIONAL PARK SERVICE)

during the Civil War. More than 500,000 were killed outright or died of wounds or disease. About 360,-000 of these dead were Union soldiers or sailors and about 160,000 were Confederates. Thus the Civil War claimed more American lives than any other war from the Revolution through Vietnam. The total financial cost of the war for both sides has been estimated at $15 billion.

The last Union veteran of the Civil War was Albert Woolson of Duluth, Minnesota, who died on August 2, 1956, at the age of 109. The last Confederate veteran was 117-year-old Walter Williams of Houston, Texas, who died on December 19, 1959.

Because of Grant's generosity, no punitive action was ever taken against Lee or any of his command. But Lee had lost his citizenship when he had volunteered to lead the Confederate armies, and it was not restored until the United States Congress gave its approval on July 22, 1975. Lee had requested the restoration of his citizenship in 1865 and had signed an oath of allegiance to the United States, but this oath had been lost among Civil War records for 110 years.

The Union victory firmly established that no state could secede from the United States or nullify a Federal law. The tragic conflict's greatest accomplishment, however, was the legal abolition of slave labor in the United States, except as punishment for a crime, which occurred with the passage of the Thirteenth Amendment to the United States Constitution on December 18, 1865.

Bibliography

An excellent but apparently little-known source for Civil War material is a series of pamphlets, *Tales of Old Fort Monroe.* This series can be purchased for a nominal fee from the Fort Monroe Casement Museum, Fort Monroe, Virginia, and makes stimulating supplementary reading in or out of the classroom.

The most clearly written, concise history of not only the Civil War but also of all America's wars through Korea appears in the Department of the Army's *American Military History, 1607–1958.* This is an ROTC manual, No. 145–20, and is available through the Superintendent of Documents, U.S. Government Printing Office, Washington, D.C.

For a somewhat more advanced yet equally concise and considerably more dramatic account of the Civil War as well as most other American wars, Robert Leckie's single-volume history, *The Wars of America* (New York: Harper & Row, Publishers, 1968), cannot be surpassed.

Civil War "buffs" young or old who wish to maintain a continuing interest in the conflict should consider subscribing to the *Civil War Times Illustrated.* This is a monthly magazine published at 206 Hanover St., Gettysburg, Pa.

The best short histories of the Civil War for more advanced readers are *The American Heritage Short History of the Civil War,* by Bruce Catton (New York: American Heritage Publishing Co., Inc., 1960), and *A Short History of the Civil War,* by Fletcher Pratt (New York: William Morrow & Co., 1935). The Pratt book was originally published under the title *Ordeal by Fire.* Both books are available in various paperback editions.

The following is also recommended for advanced readers:

Battles and Leaders of the Civil War, 4 vols. (Secaucus, N.J.: Castle Books; New York: A. S. Barnes & Co., Inc.; New York: Thomas Yoseloff, Inc., 1956). These first-hand accounts of the Civil War were first published by the old *Century* magazine immediately after the war and have since appeared in several collections. A single-volume edition was selected and edited by Ned Bradford and published by Appleton-Century-Crofts, Inc., New York, in 1956.

Other books for advanced readers include:

Berky, Andrew S., and Shenton, James P., eds. *The Historians' History of the United States,* 2 vols. New York: G.P. Putnam's Sons, 1966.

Bishop, Jim. *The Day Lincoln Was Shot.* New York: Harper & Brothers, 1955.

Boatner, Mark M., III. *The Civil War Dictionary.* New York: David McKay Co., Inc., 1959.

Catton, Bruce. *Mr. Lincoln's Army.* New York: Doubleday & Co., Inc., 1951.

————. *Centennial History of the Civil War,* 3 vols. New York: Doubleday & Co., Inc., 1961, 1963, 1965.

————. *Grant Moves South.* Boston: Little, Brown and Co., 1960.

————. *Grant Takes Command.* Boston: Little, Brown and Co., 1968, 1969.

Cooke, Alistair. *America.* New York: Alfred A. Knopf, Inc., 1973.

Foote, Shelby. *The Civil War, A Narrative,* 3 vols. New York: Random House, Inc., 1958, 1963, 1974.

Freeman, D. S. *Lee's Lieutenants,* 3 vols. New York: Charles Scribner's Sons, 1942–46.

Grant, U. S. *Personal Memoirs of U.S. Grant.* Cleveland: The World Publishing Co., 1952. This book has appeared in many editions, but the one listed has an introduction and valuable footnotes by E. B. Long, outstanding authority on the Civil War.

Long, E. B. *The Civil War Day by Day.* New York: Doubleday & Co., Inc., 1971.

Nevins, Allan. *Ordeal of the Union,* 8 vols. New York: Charles Scribner's Sons, 1947–71. This book may tell even a Civil War buff far more about the war than he cares to know, but it is nonetheless on the way to becoming a classic in its field.

Sherman, W. T. *Memoirs of Gen. W. T. Sherman,* 2 vols. New York: Jenkins & McCowan, 1890.

Van Doran Stern, Philip. *Robert E. Lee, The Man and Soldier.* New York: Crown Publishers, Inc., 1963.

Weigley, Russell F. *History of the United States Army.* New York: The Macmillan Co., 1967.

Williams, K. P. *Lincoln Finds a General,* 4 vols. New York: The Macmillan Co., 1949–56.

Index